"BURNING INTERIORS"

"BURNING INTERIORS"

David Shapiro's
Poetry and Poetics

Edited by
Thomas Fink and
Joseph Lease

Madison • Teaneck
Fairleigh Dickinson University Press

©2007 by Rosemont Publishing & Printing Corp.

All rights reserved. Authorization to photocopy items for internal or personal use, or the internal or personal use of specific clients, is granted by the copyright owner, provided that a base fee of $10.00, plus eight cents per page, per copy is paid directly to the Copyright Clearance Center, 222 Rosewood Drive, Danvers, Massachusetts 01923. [978-0-8386-4155-2/07 $10.00 + 8¢ pp, pc.]

Associated University Presses
2010 Eastpark Boulevard
Cranbury, NJ 08512

The paper used in this publication meets the requirements of the American National Standard for Permanence of Paper for Printed Library Materials Z39.48–1984.

Library of Congress Cataloging-in-Publication Data

"Burning Interiors" : David Shapiro's poetry and poetics / edited by Thomas Fink and Joseph Lease.
    p. cm.
  Includes bibliographical references and index.
  ISBN-13: 978-0-8386-4155-2 (alk. paper)
  ISBN-10: 0-8386-4155-5 (alk. paper)
  1. Shapiro, David, 1947—Criticism and interpretation. I. Fink, Thomas. II. Lease, Joseph.
  PS3569.H34Z58 2007
  811'.54—dc22
                                                    2006101578

PRINTED IN THE UNITED STATES OF AMERICA

Contents

Acknowledgments 7
List of Abbreviations 9

Introduction
THOMAS FINK AND JOSEPH LEASE 13

The Copy and the Model:
David Shapiro's *After a Lost Original*
PAUL HOOVER 21

Architect / House of Being
JUDITH HALDEN-SULLIVAN 31

"Not A Bridge":
Dialogue and Disjunction as Didacticism
in the Later Poetry of David Shapiro
JOANNA FUHRMAN 47

David Shapiro: New Jersey as Trope
CAROLE STONE 60

David Shapiro and Jasper Johns:
Ego in the Egoless Pie
STEPHEN PAUL MILLER 69

Shapiro's Comedic Poetics and
Its Limits in *Harrisburg Mon Amour,
or Two Boys on a Bus*
DANIEL MORRIS 88

Plays Well with Others:
The Collaborative Poetry of David Shapiro
DENISE DUHAMEL 98

CONTENTS

Written and Rewritten to Order:
The Gift of Generative Possibility
in the Work of David Shapiro
NOAH ELI GORDON   107

Shapiro's "A Man Holding an Acoustic Panel"
RON SILLIMAN   117

Uncanny Narrative in Shapiro's
A Burning Interior
THOMAS FINK   123

Distorted Figures: Mannerist Similes
and the Body in David Shapiro's Poetry
TIM PETERSON   138

"For Dust Thou Art" *(for David Shapiro)*
TIMOTHY LIU   152

House Blown Apart
JEREMY GILBERT-ROLFE   154

Afterword: The Night Sky
and to David Shapiro
JOSEPH LEASE   163

Works Cited   173
Notes on Contributors   177
Index   181

Acknowledgments

FROM THE BOOK *LATENESS* © 1977 BY DAVID SHAPIRO. FROM THE BOOK *To an Idea* © 1983 by David Shapiro. From the book *House (Blown Apart)* © 1988 by David Shapiro. From the book *After a Lost Original* © 1994 by David Shapiro. From the book *A Burning Interior* © 2002 by David Shapiro. All of the above reprinted with the permission of The Overlook Press.

Grateful acknowledgment is made to David Shapiro for permission to quote from his books, *January* (New York: Holt, Rinehart and Winston, 1965); *Poems from Deal* (New York: E.P. Dutton, 1969); *A Man Holding an Acoustic Panel* (New York: E.P. Dutton, 1971); and *John Ashbery: An Introduction to the Poetry* (New York: Columbia University Press, 1979); and to quote from the unpublished poems "Subject: A Song" and "IV."

Grateful acknowledgment is made to David Shapiro and Stephen Paul Miller for permission to quote from their unpublished play, *Harrisburg Mon Amour, or Two Boys on a Bus.*

"The Page-Turner," "Fremitus," "Two-Four Time," "The Mudguard Stroke," "A Family Slide," "Handar," from *The Page-Turner* by David Shapiro. Copyright © 1972, 1973 David Shapiro. Used by permission of Liveright Publishing Corporation.

Grateful acknowledgment is made to Charles Bernstein for permission to quote from his book, *Artifice of Absorption* (Philadelphia: Singing Horse Press, 1987).

"House Blown Apart" by Jeremy Gilbert-Rolfe was originally published as a chapter in Gilbert-Rolfe's book, *Beyond Piety: Critical Essays on the Visual Arts* (New York: Cambridge University Press, 1995). Reprinted with the permission of Cambridge University Press.

Peter Gizzi, excerpt from "It was Raining in Delft" in *Some Values of Landscape and Weather* © 2003 by Peter Gizzi and reprinted by permission of Wesleyan University Press.

Grateful acknowledgment is made to Burning Deck for permission to quote from "Rewriting the Other and the Others" in *Artificial Heart* (Providence, RI: Burning Deck, 1998).

Grateful acknowledgment is made to Michael Palmer for permission to quote from his poem "Music Rewritten" in *First Figure* (San Francisco: North Point Press, 1984).

Abbreviations

QUOTATIONS FROM DAVID SHAPIRO'S WORKS ARE CITED IN THE TEXT using the following abbreviations, followed by the page numbers. When lines are sufficiently located, no citation appears.

J	*January*. New York: Holt, Rinehart and Winston, 1965.
PFD	*Poems from Deal*. New York: E.P. Dutton, 1969.
MHAP	*A Man Holding an Acoustic Panel*. New York: E.P. Dutton, 1971.
PT	*The Page-Turner*. New York: Liveright, 1973.
L	*Lateness*. Woodstock, NY: Overlook, 1977. [unpaginated]
TI	*To An Idea*. Woodstock, New York: The Overlook Press, 1983.
HBA	*House (Blown Apart)*. Woodstock, NY: Overlook Press, 1988.
ALO	*After a Lost Original*. Woodstock, NY: Overlook Press, 1994.
BI	*A Burning Interior*. Woodstock, NY: Overlook Press, 2002.

"BURNING INTERIORS"

Introduction

Thomas Fink and Joseph Lease

> "I'm still holding out for a poetry in which meaning is discovered rather than refined, where poetry is on trial, but where the trial is sufficient unto itself, producing innovation and investigation not verdicts or conclusions."
> —Charles Bernstein, *My Way*, 29–30

THE U.S. POETRY SCENE AT THE PRESENT TIME IS FERTILE AND HETERogeneous,[1] and David Shapiro's maximalist poetics play a crucial role—Shapiro's poetry and poetics exemplify fullness, experiment, and critique. They resist dogma. Many of the most important contemporary poets situate themselves at the interstices—they place their poems between and among modes and traditions. Among those modes are Language Poetry, the Black Mountain School, the New York School, the San Francisco Renaissance, branches of the New American poetry invested in authentic "voice," sensory imagery, and natural free-verse, and surrealists transplanting early twentieth-century innovations into American idioms. The list could go on. Moreover, many of these poets explore questions of identity in their work, calling attention to the ways in which race, ethnicity, gender, sexual identity, and class demystify notions of universalizing measures of aesthetic and cultural value. When Daniel Barbiero perceives a resurgence of lyric in a "new generation of poets . . . who have . . . an understanding of the subjective as a factor dependent on social, linguistic, and other structures," he is also describing what Shapiro has been doing for forty years.[2] Shapiro's poems explore and problematize self and culture—he does put poetry on trial (in Bernstein's terms); his work discovers and resists meaning, and challenges conventional notions of fixed and commodified identity. Barbiero argues that the work of the new lyric poets "pivots on a sense of inwardness as outwardly constrained if not compromised": the fact that this could be a description of Shapiro's starting point goes a long way toward accounting for his increasing appeal to new generations of innovative poets. But one must combine Shapiro's awareness of the self as woven into language and culture with his singular musical gift.

In a 1990 interview with Joseph Lease, David Shapiro states: "My own sense is that some of us have tried to make the flux or the impressionism of the New York School into something 'solid as that of the Museums.' I often feel our task is a Cezannism of trying to fix the mere impressionistic empiricism of great poets such as James Schuyler and Frank O'Hara into something angrier, more sexual, whatever that might mean, less lenient with history."[3] If one relates the terms "anger" and "history," it seems accurate to suggest that Shapiro's overt anger about historical injustice sets him apart from his seniors in the New York School, whose "anger" about such matters is either indirect, submerged, or relatively insignificant compared with other concerns. Indeed, various essays in this book address the sociopolitical dimension of Shapiro's work. The serious reader of Shapiro's mature work will also note that such binaries as origin/copy, absence/presence, interiority/exteriority, continuity/ discontinuity, and center/periphery continually enter the texts.

Shapiro's writing has appeared in many highly visible and influential anthologies, including *The Best American Poetry 1989, 1996,* and *2004* (edited, along with guest poets, by David Lehman), *The Best of the Best American Poetry 1987–1997* (edited by Harold Bloom), *Postmodern American Poetry: A Norton Anthology, The Body Electric,* and various other collections. His work has been celebrated by an usually wide range of distinguished readers, including Bloom, Ron Silliman, Robert Creeley, Adrienne Rich, Lyn Hejinian, Andrei Codrescu, and Michael Palmer. Moreover, a new generation of poets, eager to find brilliant sources of experimentation, sees that Shapiro has long been deeply investigating linguistic and cultural representation in extraordinary poems. Shapiro's work strikes them as musical, visionary, and witty—all at once. They rightly feel that Shapiro's poetry is original, candid, philosophical, heartbreaking, and funny. The essays in *"Burning Interiors": David Shapiro's Poetry and Poetics* illuminate a useful range of major works in Shapiro's canon and raise important questions about the nature and cultural contexts of poetry that Shapiro trenchantly addresses.

In the opening essay, "The Copy and the Model: David Shapiro's *After a Lost Original*," Paul Hoover, editor of the influential *Postmodern American Poetry: A Norton Anthology* and poet of stature, ponders the dialogue between origins and copies in one of Shapiro's major books. In doing so, Hoover characterizes Shapiro's accomplishments in relation to the "postmodern lyric" and New York School writing. Hoover emphasizes that Shapiro's profound engagement with fundamental issues of representation results in a new and important kind of poetic sincerity: "I can't help thinking of David Shapiro in terms of Hölderlin, as one with the dangerous desire to unmask the world, to lay it bare. . . . He is among the poets who care too much. And that is a beautiful thing for poetry, though sometimes heartbreaking." He sees Shapiro's poetry as grounded simultaneously in self-consciousness and visionary moral seriousness.

Although Shapiro's art and cultural criticism draws on continental philosophy, prior criticism has only scantily explored the relation of his poetry to such work. In "Architect/House of Being," Judith Halden-Sullivan contributes Hans-Georg Gadamer's hermeneutic perspective to an analysis of Shapiro's verse that focuses on the architectural discourse in *House (Blown Apart)*. Halden-Sullivan considers how notions of "being," "presence," "transience," and "alterity," as well as concepts of speed and delay within a general preoccupation with temporality, inform Shapiro's poetic explorations of "house" or "home"/"homelessness." For her, the poet's refusal of transparent referentiality offers positive consequences for engagement with these philosophical problems. In terms also taken up by Tim Peterson in his essay, the problematization of the binary opposition of inside/outside is at stake here, as is the encounter between a plenitude of signification and undecidability.

Joanna Fuhrman in "'Not a Bridge': Disjunction and Dialogue as Didacticism in the Poetry of David Shapiro" identifies the transience of existence, as well as the relationship between uncertainty and the will to knowledge, as a major concern in the work. Fuhrman interrogates the intersection of disjunction and dialogue, which she views as an opportunity for perspectival shifts. She traces how Shapiro, in facing the ethical dangers of certainty, develops an important interplay between didactic and antididactic impulses, just as he charts the confrontation between descriptive and antidescriptive aims.

Acutely aware that Shapiro is a master of disjunction, Carole Stone in "David Shapiro: New Jersey as Trope" wagers an antithetical interpretation that elucidates the salience of pervasive experimentation's referential underside. Positing a sense of "home" that departs from Halden-Sullivan's, she speculates on the significance of a precise locale—where the poet spent his childhood—to his work. The title of Shapiro's second book, *Poems from Deal* (E.P. Dutton, 1969) cites a New Jersey town central to his childhood as "origin" of these "communications," and Stone indicates how such references abound in the poetry. Like Fuhrman, she is interested in the multiple perspectives afforded by dialogue, but for Stone, the pull of family ties (New Jersey) is in productive conflict with the allure of destabilizing, defamiliarizing aesthetic innovation (the New York School's New York City).

Stephen Paul Miller, on the other hand, considers in "Jasper Johns and David Shapiro: Ego in the Egoless Pie" how Shapiro's vital involvement with the visual arts has influenced his poetic development. A cultural critic and poet best known for *The Seventies Now: Culture as Surveillance* (Duke University Press, 1999), in which he develops analogies among visual art, literature, and political processes, Miller reflects on how Shapiro and Johns—in reducing the pull of the maker's intention (as self-expression, illusionistic description, or narrative) while utilizing the found or given, questioning received symbolism, underlining the distinction of signifier and signified, and emphasizing the material properties of their media—behave similarly and present parallel implications for their interpreters. Miller elucidates the impact of John Cage's poetics on both figures.

Essays by Daniel Morris and Denise Duhamel address a question that previously has not been considered in studies of Shapiro's work: How do Shapiro's own collaborations in poetry and drama respectively reflect his overall poetics, including his views about authorship/authority and intertextuality? It is important to note that Shapiro himself has written a significant essay entitled "Art as Collaboration: Toward a Theory of Pluralist Aesthetics," for the 1984 Smithsonian Institute catalogue, *The Artist as Collaborator*. Morris devotes his essay, "Shapiro's Comedic Poetics and Its Limits in *Harrisburg Mon Amour, or Two Boys on a Bus*," to an analysis of Shapiro's collaborative play with Stephen Paul Miller, written in 1979 and 1980. For him, the play evinces a poetics in which closure is distrusted intellectually and aesthetically and is linked with death and destruction, therefore dreaded—consistently deferred by comedic prolongations of shared speech. However, within the play are reminders of how accidents violently intrude and disrupt the "boys'" speculations. Dialogical interchange here is not merely a representation of two unified lyric "selves"; when the two speakers depart from a single persona and try on various "masks," the cultivation of multiplicity, according to Morris, decenters the pretensions of the authorial self. Such gestures produce similar effects to the emphasis on uncertainty that both Halden-Sullivan and Fuhrman find in Shapiro's poetry.

In "'Plays Well with Others': The Collaborative Poetry of David Shapiro," Duhamel, a poet noted for both her individual and collaborative work, examines, along with earlier collaborations with children, a group of poems *actually* authored by a father-son team. Duhamel discovers spiritual longing, wisdom, and playfulness in poems that make God a character. Roles or attitudes are not demarcated in advance, and it sometimes seems as though a third participant exists. Speaking of how similes serving as a child-like bridge from the familiar to the unfamiliar are offered as stabs at tentative explanation of difficult concepts, Duhamel notes that dialogical exploration never hardens into the dogma that mars much theologically oriented poetry.

Noah Eli Gordon meditates about ways in which other poets indicate the contours of Shapiro's achievement by "rewriting" his texts. Gordon's "Written and Rewritten to Order: The Gift of Generative Possibility in the Work of David Shapiro" uses Lewis Hyde's notion of "The Gift," adapted from Marcel Mauss's anthropological writings, as a framework for examining and elucidating the implicit reverence with which both Michael Palmer and Peter Gizzi approach Shapiro's work. He points out how Shapiro the collagist is an especially felicitous source for such revision. In Shapiro's work, a layering of significations and "dream logics" keeps the reader's sense of the poem's subject open, and this invites resourceful poet-readers to follow rhythms, diction, and syntax to "trace" one or two possibilities in the text and also to effect salient swerves.

As noted earlier, "anger" about "history" is a feature of Shapiro's work that sets it apart from much New York School writing. A Vietnam-era student protester, Shapiro was captured in a 1968 photo (first printed in *Life* magazine) in an act of political parody: smoking a cigar with his feet on Columbia University President Grayson Kirk's desk. In his interview with Joseph Lease, he speaks of "an anti-imperialistic theme" as a strain in his work that reflects "Jewish earnestness and . . . prophetic qualities in Isaiah." Ron Silliman, Thomas Fink, and Jeremy Gilbert-Rolfe consider the political "content" of particular works by this seemingly "abstract" poet, though other contributors also hint at the articulation of the social.

Ron Silliman, one of the premier poets and theoreticians of the Language avant-garde, praises Shapiro's stylistically varied, eighteen-section poem "A Man Holding an Acoustic Panel" and finds that it includes an uncanny collaging of scientific allusions, and is engaged with history and the political in subtle ways. Silliman finds an aura of the intense "shock" or "shock wave" encountered by immigrants to the U.S. in the first sections of Shapiro's poem, and further sections bring further violent reverberations. Silliman concludes his essay with an analysis of the most pointedly and poignantly political section, "The Funeral of Jan Palach," which serves as an elegy for the famous martyr in the cause of Czech liberation against Soviet control in 1969. Lines from the poem were included in John Hejduk's monument to Palach in Prague.

Having emphasized disjunction in *The Poetry of David Shapiro* (Fairleigh Dickinson University Press, 1993), Thomas Fink now uses his essay "Uncanny Narrative in Shapiro's *A Burning Interior*" as an occasion to situate the simultaneous presence of disjunction and critically acute, reinvigorated narrative possibilities in Shapiro's work. This confluence of elements serves the poet's elliptical but socially committed meditations on power relations. Fink notes that many have read early Language theory as a proscription of narrative, even if individual Language poets developed a much more nuanced, flexible sense of poetic possibilities, and that "New Narrative" writers and younger ("post-Language") poets set out to carve a space for their own discourse, in part, by challenging the alleged proscription and reimagining opportunities for narrative. He presents the example of Shapiro as a distinguished experimental poet (of the same generation as many Language writers) whose uses of narrative can provide ample sustenance for their emergent poetics.

Like Fink, Tim Peterson in "Distorted Figures: Mannerist Similes and the Body in Shapiro's Poetry" takes a particular literary strategy as a point of entry to discuss a manifestly social concern in Shapiro's writing. He calls attention to the discontinuous, digressive, and defocusing functioning of the poet's "groundless" similes and defines a line of Mannerism that stretches from Renaissance painters like Parmigianino, to the eccentric French novelist Raymond Roussel, and on to John Ashbery and finally, Shapiro. Utilizing the art historian Arnold Hauser's perspective, along with Jacques Lacan's analysis of the relation between metonymy and desire and Tenney Nathanson's account of metonymy and voice in Walt Whitman's poetry, Peterson indicates that Shapiro's similes, behaving metonymically, enact an allegory about the human body in which the boundaries of inside/outside are thoroughly disrupted. He maintains that Shapiro's poems create a rich questioning of what constitutes the body and what constitutes nature at any given point in a poem. Peterson's productive interrogation of this dynamic in his poetry both confirms Hoover's and Halden-Sullivan's insights into Shapiro's deployment of space, and places the problematic in other salient contexts.

Timothy Liu has contributed a poem, "For Dust Thou Art," which is dedicated to David Shapiro. In this three-section poem, tropes and images of textuality, sexuality, interiority/exteriority, and family make contact with various thematic and aesthetic concerns in Shapiro's poetry that are addressed in this book.

In "House Blown Apart," Jeremy Gilbert-Rolfe, a distinguished painter and art theorist, celebrates Shapiro's "scholarly" rapport with Ezra Pound's and T. S. Eliot's modernism and his regard for such cultural theorists as Hannah Arendt and Meyer Schapiro. He identifies Shapiro's ability to infuse a verbal architecture influenced by the French Symbolists, especially Stéphane Mallarmé, with a marvelous sense of play and pathos. For Gilbert-Rolfe, Shapiro's poetry responds to the pervasive debasement of public language as underpinnings for banal authoritarianisms and mere advertising for capitalist exchange by exposing the often humorous divide between word and thing, pointing to ambiguity as destabilizing the discourses of power, and providing a child's perspective, made strange by the simultaneity of detachment, as a refusal of false orders. Gilbert-Rolfe makes a subtle and important claim for Shapiro's aesthetic power, and his analysis helps to establish the poet as a bridge between Language Poetry and a new generation of lyric poets.

Joseph Lease's "Afterword: The Night Sky and to David Shapiro" playfully explores Shapiro's relation to both the radical Jewish tradition of Franz Kafka and Walter Benjamin and the innovative American tradition of Ralph Waldo Emerson and John Cage. Lease explores the force and richness of Shapiro's poetry and poetics, celebrating Shapiro as a poet whose work enacts both profound narrative and graceful abstraction.

In his interview with Lease, Shapiro declares:

> My poetry sometimes does appropriate high and low dictions and attempts to have them explode. I am very interested in seeing what one word does to another word. It is obvious when Braque uses a newspaper against a piece of paint that he's interested in dissonance. Both. I don't think it's necessary to have breakdowns in syntax because I think that collage and this form of juxtaposition and montage can occur with forms of dislocation that we can make less trivial than mere discontinuity. A lot of the collages that I do often don't announce themselves as such, as in Marianne Moore, who really is a kind of collage poet—I think 'Marriage' is one of the great collages that we have—but she was interested in the fact that collage could be a principal of continuity. . . . I do think that if you're going to give up figuration you're going to have to give an abstract work that is as good as Velázquez. I think if you're going to give up one form of storytelling you're going to have to do it in another way.

"Burning Interiors": David Shapiro's Poetry and Poetics offers a variety of approaches that, we hope, serves as a testament to David Shapiro's resistance to myriad dogmatisms and thirst for vigorous, democratic experimentation. We trust that this collection offers cogent analysis of Shapiro's increasing importance to the American poetry scene.

NOTES

1. Charles Bernstein, *My Way: Speeches and Poems* (Chicago: University of Chicago Press, 1999).

2. Daniel Barbiero, "Reflection on Lyric Before, During and After Language," in *The World in Time and Space: Towards a History of Innovative American Poetry in Our Time*, ed. Edward Foster and Joseph Donahue (Jersey City, NJ: Talisman House, 2002), 363.

3. Joseph Lease, "After the New York School." Interview with David Shapiro, *Pataphysics Magazine* 1990. 15 Sep. 2005 *http://www.pataphysicsmagazine.com/shapiro_interview.html*

The Copy and the Model: David Shapiro's *After a Lost Original*

Paul Hoover

IN "THE WORK OF ART IN THE AGE IN MECHANICAL REPRODUCTION," Walter Benjamin raised the question of authenticity in relation to the technical reproducibility of a work of art. Since the invention of the printing press, the photograph, the photocopy, and the computer, the reproducibility of the work—that is, the copy—has more allure than the original. Indeed, we have come to question the values of originality and authenticity as sentimental. Mass media prizes the momentary and trivial over the lasting and historical; surface over depth; the self-reflexive and appropriated over claims to genius; relativism to the absolute; and multiplicity (Warhol's silk-screened Jackies) and mass dissemination to the thing itself. As the authentic shifts its ground, irony becomes the dominant mode of communication, but not the sharp ironies of the industrial age. We love not the thing but the semblance of the thing. Representations not only replace the original but also take on a lyric life of their own, as indeterminacies and rifts: "To pry an object from its shell, to destroy its aura, is the mark of a perception whose 'sense of the universal quality of things' has increased to such a degree that it extracts it even from a unique object by means of reproduction."[1]

David Shapiro's *After a Lost Original* (1994) dramatizes the orphaning of the original by its copies. The situation is comparable to the relationship of word and thing after Saussure. Postmodern lyric finds its elegiac note exactly in this lost identity of word and thing, but in its yearning rescues the word as it drowns the referent. As seen in the work of Michael Palmer and David Shapiro, it's not simply the language poetry mode that does so. They share with language poetry an essentially post-imagist poetics that includes parataxis, objectivism, abstraction, and parallel and/or serial structures.

The postmodern lyric is ironic and materialist, therefore suspicious of poetic rhetoric and beauty. George Oppen called for "a sense of the poet's self among things," not the "beauty of background music and of soft lights."[2] With his feet firmly on the ground, the poet works with what he or she has: intelligence, perception, song, but not an effulgent lyricism that begs us to be moved. Oppen wrote, "It is possible to find a metaphor for anything, an analogue: but the image is encountered, not found; it is an account of the poet's perception, of the act of perception; it is a test of sincerity, a test of conviction, the rare poetic quality of truthfulness."[3] For David Shapiro, as is generally true of the New York School of poets, this sincerity involves a sense of humor, play, and shifting points of view. A plurality of worlds is present, so there is more than the image and object to consider, such as the spaces *between* things, their distances and relations, and the interruptive and misseamed discourses that help us view this multiplicity as the new naturalism. In Shapiro's poetry, it can never be trusted that one sentence will follow another logically, thematically, or tonally. Yet we feel somehow the sincerity of his discourse, that an underlying poetic logic is present:

> Does it hurt to mix yourself up with conquistadors
> So many hands, so many javelins, so many burials
> Like the photograph of an error.
> I crossed the riddle,
> Caring about the colors, water purple and orange.
> Plunging like an elevator into an envelope
> All these letters, your branches, fragrant Rhada.
> ("You are Tall and Thin," *ALO* 16)

Postmodern lyric depends on syntax, grammar, structure, the fragment, serialism, interruptiveness, palimpsest, and, most popular with innovative poets in the post-Vietnam period, use of the page as a feature of the poem's construction and design. The poet "unfinishes" a poem, releasing it from the left margin to form Mallarméan constellations of words and phrases. The allure of the found and "eaten away" text—for example, Sappho's fragments—is also strong. Thus postmodern beauty is that of the half-struck note rather than the resonant chord, John Cage's expressive but "broken" *Suite for Toy*

Piano rather than the sonorous agreement of symphony. Our lyric contract is with isolation of the individual rather than the fierce ideological certainties of community: the thread, not the fabric. Shapiro's poetry embodies this isolation, but obstinately clings to the left margin at a time when interruptiveness and nonsequitur (the New Sentence) find expression in unmoored fragments that scatter themselves about the page as a visual sign of their disconnectedness.

The plurality of worlds is a serious matter. For asserting such a reality, the philosopher Giordano Bruno was muzzled by the Inquisition and burned at the stake. But the issue of lyric finally rests on the author's insistent placing of himself at the center, or sun, of these worlds. The seventeenth-century author Fontenelle wrote in *Entretiens sur la pluralité des mondes*, "The same desire that makes a courtier want to have the most honorable place in a ceremony makes a philosopher want to place himself in the center of a world system."[4] To counter the effects of the egotistical sublime, distance is useful—in the case of lyric, intimacy at a distance—and multiple points of view. Humor also has a sobering effect on lyric ego and afflatus.

Shapiro's compositional strategy is often that of a philosophical game in which Plato's lost original and two copies—that is, the universal chair, the carpenter's, and the mind's—serve as identical nonidentities. This triple world can be located in any representation, but especially in works like Parmigianino's *Self-Portrait in a Convex Mirror* and John Ashbery's poem of the same title, which confront the issue directly. Shapiro writes of Ashbery's poem: "And so, we watch the poet use Vasari's praise of Parmigiainino's 'great art' in copying as a parodic exaltation of a reflection upon a reflection. The contemporary poet feels estranged from any simple mimesis."[5] With its original and duplicate figures, mimesis becomes contended territory and one of Shapiro's essential subjects. This is also true of the work of Barbara Guest and Mei-mei Berssenbrugge, among others, whose poetry traces the depiction of a depiction. I have commented extensively elsewhere on Guest's "Wild Gardens Overlooked by Night Lights," a replete "fable of representation" that reflects on overlapping worlds of "surface" and "fiction." Such poetry examines how we see and think. It therefore requires a complex mimesis conscious of all levels of image, word, and thing. The abstract lyrics of David Shapiro are also fables of representation. Here is his poem "*After* Asturiana" in its entirety:

> On the road to a door
> On the way to a window
>
> I saw nothing like a soul
> Only the dust in competition
>
> Lifted by the air
> That was like a sailor joking
>
> Nothing carried to nothing
> A sailor was bouncing
>
> In the world's salt: Now dance!
> Now you are dancing like the world
>
> Nothing equals nothing like a word
> I get lost and make mistakes in your grace.
> (*ALO* 15)

The poem operates as a psalmic proof or "logic." Its opening lines are descriptive, even narrative: "I saw nothing like a soul." That is, no living beings were in evidence or alternatively, in this strictly material world of absences and falling dusts, I saw nothing to prove the existence of a soul. To substantiate my own reality as a teller, I will report that I was traveling here and there, in the essentials of life as one does, especially in the realm of the Spanish (Asturian) metaphysical. The first five lines have the steadiness and gravity of traditional lyric mode, but interference arrives with the simile "That was like a sailor joking." The unexpectedness of the comparison breaks with lyric gravity and announces the author's freedom to wink as he will. This is not a minor point. The author's shadow upon the text shifts and refocuses the poem toward its true themes: the weight of language and the "weight" of the world as absence and presence. An earthy human figure, a sailor, "bounces" into the uninhabited, objectivist world of the poem. He bounces in the world's salt, against the landscape of "Nothing carried to nothing." The earth is materially dust and more dust, the everyday shifting of minutiae that is easily prized as "nothing." But there has been an awakening, with the result that "you are dancing like the world." The world is dust until the imagination perceives its value. The situation is reminiscent of Wallace Stevens's "pressure of reality" and "pressure of imagination," as outlined in

"The Noble Rider and the Sound of Words": "It is not an artifice that the mind has added to human nature. The mind has added nothing to human nature. It is a violence from within that protects us from a violence without. It is imagination pressing back against the pressure of reality."[6]

The world is the great dancer because it is always in movement. Because the world is filled, and worlds overlay worlds within and beyond it, nothingness is primarily a projection of mind. But "nothing" is also powerful as a poetic and psychological concept, as when the empty space between things appears as an event or "thing." This is the amusement of the line "Nothing carried to nothing," which invites us to play the game of absence-presence. Nothing must be transformed to a something in order to be carried, and nothing must also become a presence or place in order to receive it. Even "nothing," the word, is something.

The most intriguing line in "After *Asturiana*" is "Nothing equals nothing like a word" (*ALO* 15). We know that a word is a good deal more than nothing. It has weight of meaning and force of intention. It can strike blows. But its only physical substance is its weight in ink. Because analogies require four figures, the assertion teeters. Nothing equals nothing like a word equals what? And what does a word equal, the thing it names? A feather doesn't "equal" the word feather, and one nothing has a different weight and function than the next one. Our nothings are emotional assertions.

Shapiro uses an absence-presence conundrum in the poem "In Germany," which directly precedes "After *Asturiana*":

> We are the sculptors now, making our own doors
> The words remain, but the gods are gone for good
>
> The idea remains, but the words are gone like gods.
> (*ALO* 14)

The gods depart through doors we ourselves have made. Only the words remain, and when the words depart, the idea remains. Such departures should be haunting, but the tease of the lyric is toward the game itself rather than toward melancholy. Shapiro's poems therefore strike me as comedies (as well as fables) of representation. They don't present a meaningless world or language. Rather, they show how complex meaning is. Hölderlin, on the other hand, depicted the tragedy and dislocation of the gods' departure. Man is homeless and "No sign/binds." In that condition of meaninglessness, there's no glass to contain him.

The title poem of his collection *To an Idea* also involves an absence-presence puzzle. I've chosen this relatively short poem so that it also can be presented in its entirety:

> I wanted to start *Ex Nihilo*
> I mean as a review of sorts.
> It's too much of a burst for some,
> Too unanalyzably simple for others,
> As one called perspective that vicious
> Doctrine, but is it: to know nothing,
> To taste something, dazzled by absence,
> By your chair, by the chair of Salome?
> Or yet another familiar dedication:
> To an idea, writ in water,
> To wild flesh, on the surface alone.
> To you who carried me like mail
> From one house to another.
> Now the cars go past the lake, as if copying could exist.
> The signs shine, through the Venetian blinds.
>
> (*TI* 15)

The poem begins as a romp, but its idea, the word "idea," is far too resonant and grave for the antic tone to survive. By the time we reach line ten, "To an idea, writ in water," the poem has become a passionate announcement of being. At the level of the surface, in daily time and place, we are wild flesh—that is, inhabitants of a real world where things live, cast shadows of their own, and die. Is "you" an idea who "carried me like mail / from one house to another" or Shapiro's own mother, his lost original, who died before the appearance of *Lateness* (1977)?

The notion of addressing an idea is amusing. What idea? And what do we mean by idea, since it has so many meanings: the original Greek *ideein*, meaning to see or conceive; concepts that result from thinking or invention; or the Platonic concept of form or universal shape now occupied by the word "ideal"? In the Platonic context, the word suggests the ennobled original of anything, which must inevitably be diminished or lost by means of its copies. The idea is a generative figure to which we can never return. We must live in the world of the copy, while the idea, or original, dwells in a resistance-less Eden. A review called *Ex-Nihilo* is comically appropriate. Ideas come out of nothing, taste like something, and dazzle us with their absence. According to the Platonic model and John Keats, meaning is written on water. The cars that pass the lake are seen on the water's surface as copies, but they are also, we know, the beautiful. The "real" cars are ordinary. It's the reflection of those cars, interrupted by wavelets, that suggests the universal. Copying does exist, for which we should be grateful. The art of life is largely in the quality of our acts of mimesis. These signs shine forth, or make an appearance, which reminds us that the word "shine" comes from the German *schein*, meaning seem. Such signs "*mach shau*," or make show, for the delight of our eyes. Moreover, "the signs shine, through Venetian blinds," the latticework of which affects our way of seeing. Our point of view is from inside the cave, and the signs project toward us. The blinds both enhance and defamiliarize what is seen, like a scene from the Robbe-Grillet novel *Jalousie*.

In the poem "You are Tall and Thin," Shapiro changes his dialectic to being and seeming. This is expressed through a game of simile, which is to say, identity and difference. All stanzas but one make use of the word "like," sometimes unobtrusively ("You are tall and thin / like your mother") and sometimes arbitrarily ("Plunging like an elevator into an envelope"). The poem concludes:

> You are a high and delegate authority
> like a lake.
> The night dies like a ninny on the wall.
>
> At night you burn like the library of Alexandria.
> In the morning you are Alexandria, in a mirror.
>
> You are so black you are white, like a firefly in sunlight.
> (*ALO* 16)

The stanzas comprise a *wunderkammern* of the use and misuse of that suspect device, the simile. William Carlos Williams wrote: "Poetry should strive for nothing else, this vividness alone, *per se*, for itself. The realization of this has its own internal fire that is 'like' nothing. Therefore, the bastardy of the simile. That thing, the vividness which is poetry by itself, makes the poem. There is no need to explain or compare. Make it and it is a poem."⁷ Shapiro is not concerned with the correct use of technique, but rather in playing a game of resemblance. After all, his seniors include John Ashbery, whose war chest includes disapproved techniques like cliché, bathos, bombast, and false-bottomed assertions. Like Ashbery, Shapiro can also surrender himself to lyric sincerity. This becomes clear in the poem's last three lines, which take on an unexpected grandeur, accuracy, and seriousness.

The transformation of the ridiculous into the sublime is a major practice of the New York School, especially in the work of Koch and Ashbery. In a parody of Elizabeth Barrett Browning's "How do I love thee?" Koch's "To You" compares the search for love to the solving of a murder case.⁸ The logic of Koch's poem is askew and its development surrealist, but it's exactly by such ludic means that he brings the poem to lyric sincerity. Much of Ashbery's poetry relies on a similar dialectic. "A Blessing in Disguise," from the early volume *Rivers and Mountains*, parodies the overwrought rhetoric of bad love poetry.⁹ But its ultimate report is one of exaltation and lyric sweep rather than comedy and bathos. Koch and Ashberry desire a full range of poetic expression—that is, by love and generosity. This generosity is also true of the work of Shapiro. He lacks their compositional easefulness, ready humor, and sweep, largely because his movements are often anxiously inward. He also carries with him the burden of a lost paradise, his former identity as a violin prodigy, a subject he treats in "Falling Upwards," one of his most personal poems:

> What was there to do? It is said it is the violinists who do not sleep.
> What was there to do? It is said we think and don't think; we are asleep.
> What was there to do? It is said music sinks into the mire up to its neck,
>   wants to crawl out, but cannot.
> What was there to do? It is said the violin was a swan, seized the boy,
>   falling upwards to some height above the earth.
>
>   (*TI* 11)

The poem is unusual in his work for its directness and steadiness of discourse. It takes the form of a fable, but not one of representation. It's about a boy who is mired up to his neck in music and desperately wishes to fly away in the beak of his beloved violin, which is also a swan and a god named Zeus. It is an ecstatic decision to be free of "life in quarter tones" and "repetitions to be sharpened." Curiously, however, the flight to freedom is described as a fall, which suggests a loss of grace or failure. The ecstasy is tinged with guilt; nevertheless there is an escape, both in the fable and in Shapiro's own life.

In an interview with Joanna Fuhrman, Shapiro described his decision to leave music:[10]

> When I give poetry readings it is very hard because I tend to see them as little encore pieces and don't play the concerto. Or I am very worried about boring people with an adagio. Charles Bernstein said, "What's wrong with boring people?" But as a violinist, I hate to see the woman in furs yawning, as I once saw when I was giving a concert at the Brooklyn Academy of Music. I was playing "Gypsy Airs" by Sarasate, and it's very hard and very flashy and the woman in furs was yawning and I thought, "OK, I am giving up music." But I haven't given up music because poetry is music, and I don't care about parts of the audience falling asleep.

I can't help thinking of David Shapiro in terms of Hölderlin, as one with the dangerous desire to unmask the world, to lay it bare. Yet his style is "difficult" and intense, as if he's drilling in rock, in a room filled with powdered stone. He is among the poets who care too much. And that is a beautiful thing for poetry, though sometimes heartbreaking. Most certainly there is darkness and a feeling of urgency that is rarely given release by the poems. The surfaces of his poems are jittery, the passageways well below ground. He has compared one of his youthful styles of poetry with the art of Jasper Johns: "I constantly was changing from one style to another. One thing I liked was the melancholy of John's smallest light bulbs. I wanted a poetry, and I think I still do, that would be as melancholy, dense, and severe as that. I wanted a poem that would somehow emit that kind of darkness."[11]

In an interview with John Tranter, Shapiro said, "My personal tendency is to be beyond myself, to look at the venetian blinds."[12] When Tranter asked if he meant, "to look out through the venetian blinds," he responded: "No, to be stopped by the venetian blinds, with hopefully snow falling behind them. And New York—I think it is important that the urban situation does give—in the last thirty years—a tremendous sense of speed, of a matrix, of Broadway Boogie-Woogie, of what elated Mondrian.... But the despair is ... a century, as Frank O'Hara said, that's too entertaining, the New York that drains one into whimsy, and that produces a poetry that looks like a minor game. I have a friend who says that art is not a game, and as a Wittgensteinian I think, well, it looks like one." There is little whimsy in Shapiro's work. Like John Ashbery, he plays the major game, which is consciousness.

Notes

1. Walter Benjamin, *Illuminations* (New York: Schocken Books, 1969), 223.
2. George Oppen, *Selected Poems* (New York: New Directions, 2003), 175, 173.
3. Ibid., 175.
4. Bernard le Bovier Fontenelle, *Conversations on the Plurality of Worlds*, trans. H. A. Hargreaves (Berkeley: University of California Press, 1990), 117.
5. David Shapiro, *John Ashbery: An Introduction to the Poetry* (New York: Columbia University Press, 1979), 7.
6. Wallace Stevens, *The Noble Rider and the Sound of Words* (New York: Vintage Books, 1951), 36.
7. William Carlos Williams, *Imaginations* (New York: New Directions, 1970), 247.
8. Kenneth Koch, *Selected Poems* (New York: Random House, 1985), 8.
9. John Ashbery, *Rivers and Mountains* (New York: Holt, Rinehart and Winston, 1967), 26.
10. Joanna Fuhrman, "Pluralist Music: An Interview with David Shapiro," *Rain Taxi Online* (Fall 2002). http://www.raintaxi.com/online/2002fall/shapiro.shtml.
11. Ibid.
12. John Tranter, "David Shapiro in Conversation with John Tranter," New York, 15 February 1984. *Jacket* 23 (August 2003). http://jacketmagazine.com/23.

Architect / House of Being

Judith Halden-Sullivan

"You have written in the shape of a house."
—"The Cup in Architecture," David Shapiro,
House (Blown Apart), 18

"I'm in the remembrance / movement and poetry
/ is fire in the house"
—"Voice," Shapiro, *After a Lost Original*, 55

"And so the snow fell
And covered up the snow and a house within."
—"A Song for Rudy Burckhardt," Shapiro,
Burning Interior, 94

For innovative poet David Shapiro, home is an elusive, amorphous address. In ontological drifts deeply anchored in the ontic, he makes present for readers the experience of being-in the-world. He reveals human openness in its manifold receptivity as the architect of an ordinary "house" in which dwells strangeness that almost defies articulation. Hans-Georg Gadamer describes such a space as "poetic dwelling": "a creative event in which mortals draw near the advent of their being."[1] Shapiro's "events" are enigmatic collages of surreal dimensions that challenge the most attentive reader. Shapiro's foremost critic and astute reader, Thomas Fink, acknowledges the undecidability that distinguishes the unfolding of Shapiro's universe, noting as paramount Shapiro's "negative scrutiny of referentiality's assertions of stable ground."[2] However, the "ground" for meaningful contexts *does* appear in Shapiro's poetry, but only to recede or morph into opportunities for multiple contradictory meanings: things change. In his essay, "On the Contribution of Poetry to the Search for Truth," Gadamer offers this description of the poem that may accurately contextualize Shapiro's innovation:[3]

> A genuine poem . . . allows us to experience "nearness" in such a way that this nearness is held in and through the linguistic form of the poem. What is the nearness that is held there? Whenever we have to hold something, it is because it is transient and threatens to escape our grasp. In fact, our fundamental experience as beings subject to time is that all things escape us, that all the events of our lives fade more and more, so that at best they glow with an almost unreal shimmer in the most distant recollection. But the poem does not fade, for the poetic word brings the transience of time to a standstill.

No contemporary poet more elegantly captures for readers the experience of Gadamerian transience than David Shapiro. He is the master-builder of such transience, constructing the house of being without a blueprint: "A map dropped from my hands / And a voice cried, From now on / You will proceed in darkness," the speaker of "Doubting the Doubts" declares, "We do not know now and we will never know" (*HBA* 59). Lack of certainty, however, does not undo either the poet's or reader's negative capability, as each of Shapiro's poems enacts moments of thought in the face of, indeed immersed in, the world's kaleidoscopic mutability. Such immersion, in Gadamer's terms, bespeaks not the experimental fringe but *the center* of thinking, evoking "nearness" to being in thought. Tradition—in particular referentiality—on the other hand, reveals the structured periphery of a "fallen" world, to employ Martin Heidegger's term, a world reduced in its reified accretion of knowledge.[4] In describing Shapiro's phenomenological poetics, this essay will examine how, then, the dialectic between the innovative and the traditional is resituated. Gadamer's aesthetics best contextualize how Shapiro reconfigures the ground of verse: a locus at once situated but not coercive, absorbed in the immediacy of the other manifest in the event of language. In particular, Gadamer's poetics of nearness more precisely articulates the ways in which Shapiro's innovative verse transcends traditional notions of *time*, reinvigorates traditional notions of *presence*, and reconstitutes *the alchemy of reading*.

What is the character of that nearness to being in thought that Shapiro makes available in his verse? The first distinctive feature in Shapiro's world-building—that to which readers are drawn near—is a vibrant, complex surplus of thingliness, an animation of the stuff of "life itself," or what Nathan Hauke calls "joyful inclusiveness."[5] Fink notes Shapiro's affinity with John Ashbery, about whom Shapiro has written extensively, apparent in their common acknowledgment of the "importance of 'the tangibility of the word.'"[6] Perhaps Shapiro is also akin to another iconoclast, Charles Olson, who claimed that to be a poet, the thinker must achieve an *humilitas*[7] standing out in relation to things; the poet must acknowledge her/his human position as a being among other beings, without privileged rank. Concrete anchors in lived experience persist, but what is curious in verse as strange and surreal as Shapiro's is the repetition of "tangibles." Four words in particular pervade his anthologies: "house," "bed," "snow," and "architecture." Other architectural terms are common, such as "roof," "walls," and "windows," even cheap container or packing materials like "cardboard." Rhetorical and poetic "architectures," forms such as analogy, parody, and elegy, and personifications of devices and genres such as "Irony," "Metaphor," "Pathos," "Comedy," and even "Criticism" itself are alive in Shapiro's texts. Categories of artistic construction—of thought—hold parity with the mundane constructs of daily life; the ontic and ontological collide and coalesce, a blurring of boundaries in the world "between signifier and signified, between a name and its object," Shapiro notes, not in regard to his own styling but to that of Stephane Mallarmé in *Poets and Painters*.[8]

There is in Shapiro's world-building commodious spaciousness that pulsates—an expansion and contraction, like respiration, from ontic to ontological proportions. For example, "the lost golf ball," lamented in the poem of the same title is, "Like a star lost on a white ceiling," alluded to as one of the "Parts of the universe" that is "missing" (*HBA* 35); the mundane yawns to remark the cosmic in a single breath. The house's ceiling—where stars are pinpointed as on a child's map of the night sky—and the sprawl of the universe seem interchangeable. And in yet another instant, "The title itself is a ceiling for / stars that shine at night, will not fade." Now the materials of the earth, the sky, and the agency of intellect (the poem's title) are bound in mutuality, much like the body and the world in "Limits": "Think of the optic nerve / Connected to everything, in a sense" (*HBA* 16). In such a polysemous space, "You have made my room a universe," the speaker declares—perhaps of the transformative power of art itself (*HBA* 36).

Conversely, the celestial universe delineated in bold primary colors in a later poem, "Multiple Suns," personifies human feelings, aspirations, and frailties: "The red sun loves to perform in front of others," and the self-satisfied green sun "is happier than ever, in certitude and size" (*ALO* 75). While the blue sun "attacks all others in a language of brilliant *passado*," our own solar system's yellow sun—a quietly questioning sun that, much like the world itself, withholds expression and "explains nothing" publicly (*ALO* 75)—"slipped away and was quiet for a billion years or so" (76). The manifold texture of Shapiro's milieu provokes synesthesia, as "one feels seeing and sees feeling" ("Limits," *HBA* 16) and light itself becomes "audible" in "The Heavenly Humor" (*PFD* 20). The repetition of Shapiro's "tangibles," however, do not at all offer thematic unity, as Fink notes in *The Poetry of David Shapiro*.[9] Instead, they provide architectural linchpins, of a sort: they constellate readers' experiences, lending in their sensuality the feel of a context without a fixed identity or with an identity that distends to a surplus of its constituent parts. They also bespeak the transience of thought as it interpenetrates the world: a temporality that distinguishes the being of the poem itself.

For Gadamer, the poem has a unique relationship to *time*: it is a temporal event that in itself can slow the transience of time by engaging readers in thought. According to Gadamer, in the face of transience, the human being's task in life is to slow down, "to make ourselves at home" amidst the profusion of impressions the world affords us."[10] However, the poem as an event "stands over and against this process like a mirror held up to it," showing not so much the world, but our immersion in the moment of thought, "this nearness in which we stand for a while."[11] The poem is an experience that deliberately slows readers to bring them nearer to what slips away: being, particularly those nuances of strangeness that both define daily experience in the world and yet elude the detection of preoccupied readers. Poems slow transience to awaken us from our complacent enchantment with the "fallen" world; they surprise us with our own condition.

Nowhere is the deliberate strangeness of this surprise more apparent than in Shapiro's sequence of poems entitled "House (Blown Apart)," in the book of the same title. The coupling of abstraction and mundanity in this collection demonstrates Gadamer's sensibility about the poem's ability to lay hold of the transience of temporal existence. Each piece in "House (Blown Apart)" unfolds an elastic thinking of worlds that asks readers to *slow down*. One way in which this is enacted is by the dense thingliness of expression: the same collection of familiar objects pervades the fourteen pieces of this section, drawing attention to the need for their reconsideration from poem to poem, for a return, for a pause. The speaker begins in "bed," recounting time past: "I can see the traces of old work / Embedded in this page, like your bed / Within a bed." (15). The persona commits to deliberately "understand material, raw / Material. . . ," to delve into origins, even to constitute human existence as building materials—"a house without windows"—human being as a locus of familiarity (home) but never easily transparent—in its simplest form reduced to "a red stain" (15), an organic smear.

Consideration of the body and its connections to worlds in lived experience continues in the next poem in this sequence, "Limits," where the speaker remarks skin as the boundary between worlds: to be the "curator" of that boundary, one must know "the inside of the body": "Think of the optic nerve / Connected to everything" (16). Inside and outside—one wanting the other—these are the erotics of worldly emplacement seen throughout Shapiro's canon. The next poem in this sequence, "The Cup in Architecture," posits a mundane household vessel as the receptacle for every possible permutation of human speculation: the cup as broken—is it evidence of a larger disruptive plot or coup? And, simultaneously, in its demotic identity, does it really demand glue? The cup morphs into attitudes and stances: "the cup as apology, and the cup without doubts" (17). The cup becomes so engorged with overdetermined, boorish certainty that "It criticizes your work," a "finite" measure of all things. Indeed, the misled "you" chided in the poem has forgotten that the cup was not so finite and that, as a matter of fact, the cup has wildly variable contexts for being—ever changing its proportions in "its nomad margins." The cup becomes a problem in need of questions and analogies. It defies certainty which itself becomes emblematized as a "broken cup"—a vessel that will not hold. The speaker boldly inquires, "What are you thinking of that is not the broken cup?" (18).

In a Heisenbergian world devoid of certainty, we can only consume "the word," an inexact referent for Shapiro, not the undistilled "elixir" of life itself, a promise of eternity, that we would choose to retain in a cup if we could; instead, we can maintain only desire, the "thirst for the broken cup" (18). We only have words "written in the shape of a house," with the pronounced barriers of "inside" and "outside." The cup is relegated "to the pavement," to the foundation of things which, curiously, is both rock and sky: "in stars and stone," both on the ground and, within that ground, that which anchors the height of possibilities for sky. But in such a locale, miraculous things can happen: as "you" seek out the familiar, "you cure a lame old man and give / him a house." The "you" addressed is capable of Christ-like healing but also feels compelled to constrain the subject of miracles in a familiar structure, the ever-present house with boundaries, the amorphous shape of being—under house arrest, as it were.

Shapiro captures those hard-won, transient moments of immersion in thought, shadowed with the realization that, to reiterate Gadamer, "all things escape us." Even "The Blank Wall" of "House (Blown Apart)" configures a double-blind behind which there is nothing, "not even the broken cup" (19). However, Shapiro intrudes upon what may seem relativist resignation to allow this affirmation: "Long live the instant," as the speaker of "Long Live the Snowflake" declares in *A Burning Interior* (13). An instant proffers a universe of time for change. Perhaps the fourteen distinct yet ontically linked constructs of "House (Blown Apart)" *each* exhort readers in the act of thinking to "change your life fourteen times":

> You must convert resolve revolutionize your dissolves.
> You might change life itself. And you might change.
> You must change. You must not outlive your life.
> ("Archaic Torsos," *HBA* 28)

Here the spectacle of transience is a wake-up call to action—to live. But the instant of "now" is never to be reduced for Shapiro: it is a complex collage of distant pasts. In "Long Live the Snowflake," the body again is a "house," with a commodious welcoming "double foyer," warmed in (yet again) a bed carved from the ages "of the oaken earth." The speaker wishes longevity for the "catachresis / Of our lives"—wishes well to those beings *living paradoxically* in the *wrong* place, given their aspirations for certainty, but in the *same* experience of time: simultaneously, whether it be in both "New Jersey / and Troy" (*BI* 13). Poetry shelters place and time—and the transience of both. "Long live the interruption / of this fragile art": poetry captures and yet explodes the moment—constructs the house and blows it apart.

Gadamer asserts, "the poetic word brings the transience of time to a standstill."[12] But, in that moment, never does Gadamer imply that presence mediated in language is unproblematic. Given presence so ontically variegated, multidimensional, and elusive as in Shapiro's poetry, Shapiro seems to concur with Gadamer. Fink affirms throughout his studies Shapiro's "skepticism about narration and transparent 'referentiality',"[13] and, for the poet's readers, this can mean a struggle in comprehending the unexpected. As Fink asserts,[14] even if open-minded readers relinquish the "hunt" for referentiality, they will

> have immense difficulty not being "seduced" occasionally to resume the hunt—"seduced" by the notion that signifiers seem at times to be pointing strongly at determinate signifieds. Language can sometimes approach the abstract condition of wordless music or the abstract materiality of paint in—let's say— abstract-expressionist art of the 1950s, but it does not go the whole distance. Hence, even if the reader senses that a poem should not be read for referential "content," s/he will probably do so at points in the reading process and then be "slapped" by an antimimetic movement in the poem. While the text never emerges as "readable" in a traditional sense, it is always hovering near the threshold of readability.

Reading Shapiro's verse may indeed seem an excursion to the fringe —the "threshold"—of decidability; language, as an adequate mediator for the world, seems to fall short.

"After *Asturiana*" seems to remark this skepticism, as the persona proclaims that, "Nothing equals nothing like a word" (*ALO* 15). Next to "After *Asturiana*" in the same book, "In Germany" contextualizes the fleeting trace of thought in language in terms reminiscent of Martin Heidegger's four-fold (earth-sky; humans-gods): "We are the sculptors now, making our own doors / The words remain, but the gods are gone for good / The idea remains, but the words are gone like gods" (14). Loss, disconnection, uncertainty. Carl Whithaus affirms this sense of failure, noting that, for Shapiro, "language and poetry always attempt to refer the reader to something even if they are not successful. It is the attempt at reference and the acknowledgment of the inevitable loss that occurs when this attempt is made that distinguishes Shapiro's works."[15]

Shapiro's "Wild Sonnet" enacts Whithaus's description. Two familiar personae who frequent Shapiro's verse and animate the "Wild Sonnet" are "the architect and the poet" (*BI* 61). The contiguity of these two professions is one undoubtedly personal for Shapiro, himself a poet who is married to an architect. But within the context of "Wild Sonnet," the pairing of poet and architect pose questions of relatedness beyond private associations. Obviously, both are makers: both build structures that stand alone and apart from their creators, held together by internally precise and contextually appropriate dynamic tensions. Both poetry and architecture can be integral units in a collection or community—in constant dialogue with surroundings they complement. Both creators, poet and architect, must understand and select their materials well; their constructs derive from the lived experience of raw earth, be it the steel of skyscrapers or the images made manifest in ink. Both poet and architect build worlds meaningful to others, perhaps even beyond the creators' intentions; both construct dwellings for thought and action.

The dialogue in "Wild Sonnet" between the two professions is mediated by either the poet herself/himself or by an unknown third party facile in the "fragile art." The speaker decides that "a cartoon," yet another medium, might be the most effective for explaining poetry to the architect. This seems sensible: architects embody ideas in shapes and know well the meaning of dimensions, and so are suitable readers for a panel of pictures such that a cartoon might pose. But the construct of the cartoon as indicative of the art of verse-making is enigmatic at best. A cat—an animate, instinctive being not particularly known for deliberate thought—casts "psychology" and "gifts"—narratives of emotions and motives? pleasing forms?—into a river intended for unknown others at a great distance. The "pronoun in its cell"—the unspecified representative of an actor or that which belongs to such an actor (a possessive pronoun)—is constrained in a secluded location but is alive and well until "released to the world," where the pronoun is particularized as a gendered, unnamed "her" and "she" who withers from infectious exposure (61). Distance and obscurity mark the mediation evoked in "Wild Sonnet": the uncertain identity of the speaker who instructs the architect, the strangely evocative cartoon characters, and the pronoun disintegrating without a referent. Is this the distinction of Shapiro's poetic legacy—a nearness to loss? I think not. In "Wild Sonnet," the splicing of the ontic entities of lived experience within a surreal narrative that parallels the mysteries and dilemmas of the creative process actually *bespeaks the process itself.* The poetic event is intuitive and concrete, disjunctive in its sources of thought, meant for others, and yet vulnerable to their misidentifications. The world provides possibilities for presence but withholds as much as it affords. That is what it *is*, Shapiro seems to assert. Otto Poggeler describes the project of thinking the "truths" of such a world: "The thinking of the truth of Being must be understood from its own proper matter. Its task is to correspond to the presence as well as the absence in Being, to the revealing as well as the concealing, to come from the revealment which has already occurred and to take up lodging in what is concealed—not in order finally to set aside concealment, but to tend to it as that which always shelters the revealment in its inexhaustibility."[16]

Charles Olson, a fellow traveler in the pursuit of presence, attuned to the conditions of being, explains what I believe is both Shapiro's recognition *and* his Herculean task: "We are in the presence of the only truth which the real can have, its own undisclosed because not apparent character. Get [the character of the real] out with no exterior means or materials, no mechanics except those hidden in the thing itself, and we are in the hands of the mystery."[17] Shapiro, too, permits things to be *as themselves*, however overwhelming "the mystery" revealed. Shapiro's verse is an enactment of lived experience in the event of the poem—poems as "alive" as the one-of-a-kind snowflakes that persist in so many of his poems ("The Snow is Alive," *ALO* 12). "This then is a possible house," the speaker declares in the poem sequence entitled "House" in *After a Lost Original* and acknowledges that, "Yes it is all about itself" (42). Born of the contingencies of the moment, the poem *is* what it is about.

For Gadamer works of art, particularly poetry, reinvigorate traditional notions of *presence*: verse sets forth a dynamic, performative, autonomous self-presentation. Gadamer claims that "the work of art does not simply refer to something, because what it refers to is actually there."[18] The language of poetry in particular "does not intend something, but rather is the existence of what it intends."[19] It becomes an experience that the world affords; it is not merely *about* the world. "The poem," Gadamer claims, "does not stand before us as a thing that someone employs to tell us something. It stands there equally independent of both reader and poet. Detached from all intending, the word is complete in itself."[20] According to Gadamer's description, the poem occupies a unique space. While created by one being, the poem is never bound by monolithic authorial intentions.

At the same time, without need of intention, the poem sets in motion experiences of worlds, sufficient and complete in its words and their possibilities for connections with readers over time.

The words of the poem do not remark language's instability—the lost trace of meaning from the moment of utterance—but language's ineffable, inexhaustible abundance. More pointedly, for Gadamer, the poem's autonomy becomes apparent not when representation becomes transparent but only when a "disruption in communication provides a motive for reaching back to the text as the 'given'"[21]—not when matters are simple, but when they are problematic—a trait that is a hallmark of Shapiro's verse. As David Haney elaborates, "a text is more immediately present the further it departs from being a mere sign of a prior situation, a means to an end"[22]; "The autonomy of a work of art," he notes, "lies not in its separation from an original referent or from the temporality of human life but in its own kind of temporality."[23] This temporality, as noted previously, is concomitant with Gadamer's sense of the poem as an event or *experience*.

Titled like a page in a personal diary, Shapiro's poem "November Twenty-Seventh," appearing in *To an Idea* (1983), enacts an event of questioning; it is not "about" anything; on the contrary, it seems to be concerned with "nothing." In the poem, the speaker claims, "The mountain represents nothing, the mountain air / Represents nothing, but two birds seem bad enough" (*TI* 76). Indeed, the mountain does *not* represent: *it is*. It stands. The air, invisible and fresh, need *not* represent; like the mountain, *it is*. The human mode of being is cast into a world that then molds it; the world bestows upon its experiencers' manifold possibilities for presence and, at the same instant, appears to withdraw because of human beings' unidirectional, limited perceptions. But the world *is*. The world is brought nearer to people by thought, which, as Heidegger defines it, "cuts furrows into the soil of Being."[24] Language makes the world near and present, despite the slippage inherent in human mediation. The two birds included in the poem—perhaps those alluded to in the old adage, "a bird in the hand is worth two in the bush"—crystallize for readers the difficulty of grasping: perhaps the bird in hand eludes us in its ordinary strangeness, while at the same time we complacently assert that not knowing its distant avian companions seems "bad enough."

In the same manner, in "After *Asturiana*," two strong points of negation beg reconsideration. First, in line three, "I saw nothing like a soul" (*ALO* 15). A different emphasis in intonation suggests that "nothing" or absence is *like* "a soul": invisible, formless, yet metaphysically animate, and to some readers the source of eternal being. The poem brings into contiguity nothingness and being, the moment and eternity. "Nothing equals nothing like a word" may manifest the absence inherent in language, but it also affirms presence: absence ("nothing") is ("equals") nothing at all like language, "like a word." The mechanics of mediation are invisible, at once an absence that withholds the world and a presence that bestows it.

Such an event of destabilization of binary oppositions is enacted in Shapiro's poem, "A Song for Rudy Burckhardt" in *A Burning Interior*. Poetry and architecture are once again united, this time melded with the rest of worldly experience through the machinations of perhaps the most pervasive ontic entity or image in Shapiro's verse—snow. "A Song for Rudy Burckhardt" is comprised of twelve couplets, eleven of them having as their first line, "And so the snow fell," with couplet eleven emphatically expressed as "And oh the snow fell" (94). Snow, in Shapiro's world-building, demands far more attention than I will offer it here. It is "alive" ("The Snow is Alive," *ALO* 12), embodying at times, a "savage and paradoxical remark," "unique," but, in a fashion that galvanizes Shapiro's meditations, always "Copies of a copy!" ("Which Word," *HBA* 85). In "Rudy Burckhardt," snow falls in torrents that overwhelm the mundane world of experience: it "covered up poetry," cities, architecture as a generic form, even the highly evocative and generative "red orange sexual flower" that burns much like the suns bursting with plasma and angst in *After a Lost Original*. Snow envelopes poetry and even itself—"And covered up the snow and a house within" (99). This last claim returns attention to the curious nature of Shapiro's snow in that it desires a transgression impossible for its constitution but one that it strangely achieves; snow falls *inside* dwellings, as it does in "House": "Secretly snow was falling within" (*ALO* 47). In still more outlandish feats that defy its nature, the snow even piles higher than the sky, overtaking "even passing clouds" (95). Snow in its ontic character defines uniqueness: popular science asserts that no two snowflakes are alike.

In "Rudy Burckhardt," endless uniqueness embraces all: poetry, architecture, "water-towers," even mimetic representations of particular snowfalls captured in "photographs of snow" (*BI* 95). However, such uniqueness yields a vision of uniformity and consistency, intoned twelve times in a dozen couplets like a litany. Snow sprawls, but also seems sinister. While energetic and mischievous, Shapiro's snow also enshrouds the world of experience in white—bleaching primary colors—with a certainty that smothers the house of being as it coldly defines it. Unique or uniform? Are readers left with yet another "broken cup"—an emblem of uncertainty?

Always, it seems, in Shapiro's canon it is impossible to decide. What are we, as readers, left with after experiencing the event of Shapiro's poems? The speaker in "A Night of Criticism" recalls to readers that, after all, "At the end of the greatest book of poetry / all you have is a book in your hands" (*ALO* 56). The instant of utterance brings the world nearer, but readers cannot retain it like "a lost original." The poet names things only to expedite their belonging to others in the instant of reading: "one names something only not / to have it, the ruined theme of absence." "[P]oetry is not exactly affirmative," the speaker continues. It is not exact to one reader's sensibility—it is not just Shapiro's "bed"—but possibilities for its lineaments are open to all.

Poetry is not ethnography of a particular time and place, "like thick description in anthropology" that somehow seeks to determine (or overdetermine) our lives, distilled as originary moments like a child's first experience of snow. Nor is poetry "the realist in a corridor for the winter"—attempting a transitional path in intellectually Spartan surroundings, pragmatically trying, again, to correct the impossible and inevitable "swiftly falling" constructs that strive for a congruity the world cannot provide. Instead, the world is like "a cloud" (56). In our grasping, the vaporous world slips away. "In these things," the persona of "November Twenty-Seventh" declares, "there is an immense exile like a surface" (*TI* 76). Accepting superficial "surfaces" makes for our banishment from nearness. To paraphrase Charles Olson, we become estranged from that with which we should be most familiar.[25] As "November Twenty-Seventh" has it, "when we try to stop expressing it"—when we allow language to speak from the thing itself, to make present the moment—only then "words are successful" (*TI* 76). If "knowing" is the overdetermined intention of referentiality, then better that "I know that I love the verb not to know" (*TI* 75).

The nearness to being in thought that Shapiro's verse makes palpable is bold in its thingliness and patterned in its repetition of what seems idiosyncratic yet archetypal entities: house, bed, snow. Complex in its permutations and intractable, his poetry is not about something in a narrative or representational sense, but it makes manifest elastic possibilities for being-in-the-world. Yet, as one of Shapiro's personae confesses, "I've built nothing; you are the architect" (*TI* 75). "You are the you in this poem," Shapiro's speaker pronounces, ever-aware of the symbiotic relationship among the disparate, polyphonic selves of poets and readers ("You Are the You," *ALO* 33). For Shapiro's readers, the event of his verse reconstitutes *the alchemy of reading*, in particular the dialogue with "the other." While certainly, as David Haney notes, "poems are [not] equivalent to persons,"[26] Gadamer states: "the process by which the truth of a poem is revealed is instructively similar to the unconcealing that goes on in the ethical hermeneutics of being open to . . . the truth of another person."[27] And so, as Haney surmises, "engagement with a historical text can be modeled on a conversation with another person, even though texts are obviously unlike conversational partners . . . . Subjectivities are subordinated to the play of a conversation in which the truth that emerges fuses and transcends partners' individual conceptual 'horizons'."[28]

As Brice Wachterhauser notes, Gadamer is "always aware of this dialectic of individuality, identity, and difference,"[29] as is Shapiro, as the examination of "A Night of Criticism" reveals. So, like Gadamer's work of art, the poem "becomes an experience changing the person experiencing it."[30] The language of poetry delivers thinking of a world into "nearness," bringing thinkers closer to what is.[31] Gadamer explains that "the word summons up what is 'there' so that it is palpably near. The truth of poetry consists in creating a 'hold upon nearness.'"[32] The "hermeneutics of nearness," in Krzysztof Ziarek's terms, "induces language to 'pay attention' to the inscriptions of otherness, of the unsaid, in what it brings to words. In the end, at stake is not a hermeneutics of knowing or understanding but one of listening . . . of letting come into one's own—efforts summed up by the enigmatic sense of nearing. It is a hermeneutics that . . . attempts to deliver a message, to let it say itself, without covering or explaining away what remains baffling and other in it."[33] Ziarek's description aptly characterizes Shapiro's canon. Ziarek explains further that, Heidegger, later in his writing, abandoned the notion of difference and replaced it with "nearness." Difference, Ziarek explains, remains "complicitous with the dialectical sublation of otherness.... By contrast, nearness . . . underscores the rejection of domination and erasure of alterity intrinsic to difference and the attempt to circumvent the logic of objectification,"[34] an exchange of identities echoed in Shapiro's claim to build "nothing" on the one hand and his invitation to the reader to create, to become "the architect," no matter how complex the scaffolding: "The reader loses his way richly, but it is not certain that the reader / loses. / Nevertheless, you found your way about, though I do not know / you" ("Sentences," *ALO* 31).

Experimental poets like David Shapiro invite readers to participate in an experience with language that returns them to the process of being themselves—a thinking of the world of the poem and, in so doing, a "steeping oneself into the whole of creation," as Gadamer calls it, "in which we become more."[35] Shapiro asks readers to define and redefine for themselves the simplest terms of their being: their location, the address of their "house." To do so, he unravels the traditional structure of the statement to afford readers an encounter with openness that remarks their being-in-the-world, their dialogue with "the other" that constitutes the world. His poetic collages shake loose the syntax of traditional discourse in favor of an associative splicing of imagery and the nonhierarchical melding of abstract notions with concrete detail; in so doing, he posits a propositional structure in his verse only to explode it to openness beyond assertion. His canon reveals the *logos* of postmodern American innovative poetics to be nearness—not at the fringe, but the *center* of being. In particular, Gadamer's poetics of nearness best contextualizes, first, how Shapiro's verse slows time: his linguistic challenges demand new, deliberate reading strategies. These reading processes animate the character of truth as revealment in response to readers' *a priori* openness. Shapiro's experimental verse also redefines presence: it crosses borders beyond the paradigm of referential artifact to the fluidity and immediacy of an experience of nearness that "does not intend something, but rather is the existence of what it intends," to reiterate Gadamer's description. Shapiro's poetry also remakes the alchemy of reading: his poems become egalitarian partners in a transformative dialogue. In these ways, David Shapiro's own poetics of nearness instigates a remaking of the conjunctions and disjunctions between the innovative and the traditional to reveal another locus: an open space where the problematics of poetizing ontology "become thinkable."[36]

Readers' management of his ambiguity and undecidability comes to constitute a stance in relation not just to his verse but to how readers construct meaning—the mirror, as Gadamer names it, that shows the struggle to make ourselves at home within the open space that is the poem *and* our world.

Notes

1. James Risser, *Hermeneutics and the Voice of the Other: Re-reading Gadamer's Philosophical Hermenuetics* (Albany: SUNY Press, 1997), 187.
2. Thomas Fink, "David Shapiro's 'Possibilist' Poetry," *Jacket 23* (August 2003), http://www.jacketmagazine.com (accessed July 14, 2005).
3. Hans-Georg Gadamer, "On the contribution of poetry to the search for truth," in *The Relevance of the Beautiful*, trans. Nicholas Walker (Cambridge: Cambridge University Press, 1989), 114.
4. Martin Heidegger, *Being and Time,* trans. John Macquarrie and Edward Robinson (New York: Harper and Row, 1962), 264.
5. Nathan Hauke, "Meditations on David Shapiro: Memory and *Lateness.*" *Jacket 23* (August 2003), http://www.jacketmagazine.com .
6. Thomas Fink, "David Shapiro's 'Possibilist' Poetry."
7. Charles Olson, *Selected Writings of Charles Olson,* ed. Robert Creeley (New York: New Directions, 1966), 25.
8. David Shapiro, *Poets and Painters: Lines of Color* (Denver: Denver Art Museum, 1979).
9. Thomas Fink, *The Poetry of David Shapiro* (Rutherford, NJ: Fairleigh Dickinson University Press, 1993), 40.
10. Gadamer, "On the contribution of poetry to the search for truth," 114.
11. Ibid., 115.
12. Ibid., 114.
13. Thomas Fink, "David Shapiro's 'Possibilist' Poetry."
14. Thomas Fink, *The Poetry of David Shapiro,* 41.
15. Carl Whithaus, "Immediate Memories: (Nostalgic) Time and (Immediate) Loss in the Poetry of David Shapiro," *Jacket 23* (August 2003), http://www.jacketmagazine.com.
16. Otto Poggeler, *Martin Heidegger's Path of Thinking,* trans. Daniel Magurshak and Sigmund Barber (Atlantic Highlands, NJ: Humanities Press International, Inc., 1987) 223.
17. Charles Olson, *Selected Writings of Charles Olson,* 45.
18. Hans-Georg Gadamer, "The Relevance of the Beautiful," in *The Relevance of the Beautiful*, trans. Nicholas Walker (Cambridge: Cambridge University Press, 1989) 35.
19. Hans-Georg Gadamer, "On the contribution of poetry to the search for truth," 113.
20. Ibid., 107.

21. Hans-Georg Gadamer, "Text and Interpretation," in *Dialogue and Deconstruction,* eds. Diane P. Michelfelder and Richard E. Palmer (Albany: SUNY Press, 1989), 34.

22. David P. Haney, "Aesthetics and Ethics in Gadamer, Levinas, and Romanticism: Problems of Phronesis and Techne," *PMLA* 114.1 (January 1999), 39.

23. Ibid., 38.

24. Joseph Kockelmans, *On the Truth of Being: Reflections on Heidegger's Later Philosophy* (Bloomington: Indiana University Press, 1984), 161.

25. Charles Olson, *The Special View of History,* ed. Ann Charters (Berkeley: Oyez, 1970), 1.

26. David P. Haney, "Aesthetics and Ethics in Gadamer, Levinas, and Romanticism," 38.

27. Ibid.

28. Ibid., 39.

29. Brice R. Wachterhauser, *Beyond Being: Gadamer's Post-Platonic Hermeneutical Ontology* (Evanston, IL: Northwestern University Press, 1999), 48.

30. Hans-Georg Gadamer, *Truth and Method,* 2nd rev. ed., rev. trans. Joel Weinsheimer and Donald G. Marshall (New York: Crossroad, 1990), 92.

31. Hans-Georg Gadamer, "On the contribution of poetry to the search for truth," 113.

32. Ibid.

33. Krzysztof Ziarek, *Inflected Language: Toward a Hermeneutics of Nearness* (Albany: SUNY Press, 1994), 10.

34. Ibid., 11.

35. Hans-Georg Gadamer as quoted in James Risser, *Hermeneutics and the Voice of the Other: Re-reading Gadamer's Philosophical Hermeneutics* (Albany, NY: State University of New York Press, 1997), 205.

36. Krzysztof Ziarek, *Inflected Language,* 13.

"Not A Bridge":
Dialogue and Disjunction as Didacticism in the Later Poetry of David Shapiro

By Joanna Fuhrman

> And the critic cries: it is gray!
> Yes, but so is grass or your hat.
> Like a photograph of hands or a stairway,
> criticism could be like love, specific.
> —David Shapiro, "A Visit from the Past,"
> *House (Blown Apart)*, 21

As I was gathering ideas for this chapter on the recent poetry of David Shapiro, the specter of the critic in "A Visit from the Past" haunted me. Is it possible to say something about Shapiro's poetry that will not be too general? Will I be like the critic in "A Visit from the Past" who, on seeing "Mother Burning Father / in layers of newspaper" only notices "it is gray?" My hope is that by focusing on describing Shapiro's poetry instead of conceptualizing it I might avoid that critic's fate. Yet I realize that any account is by necessity a simplification. Shapiro is a particularly tricky poet to write about because his work is so conscious of the limits of description. For Shapiro, description is difficult because the world is in flux; existence is mercurial, and consequently our knowledge of it is limited. Moreover, pretending to know or be able to describe more than one actually can leads to objectification and misunderstanding of others. This awareness of the dangers of description can be seen in his use of disjunction and dialogue. The way Shapiro employs these techniques, they call into question the nature of representation even as they attempt to describe. In this way, these techniques serve not only aesthetic purposes, but moral ones as well. Shapiro's use of disjunction and dialogue reflect an awareness of the ethical dangers of certainty. Through them, he is able to write a poetry that is didactic while simultaneously reflecting an awareness of the problems of didacticism.

What I want to call the disjunctive quality of Shapiro's poetry is most obviously seen in his construction of metaphors and similes. His metaphors startle because their tenor and vehicle change as they are being developed. Instead of following an A equals B formula, the typical Shapiro metaphor follows an A equals B, which is now Q and was once Z. As his metaphors expand, they defy expectation. Flouting the dull English teacher's advice against mixed metaphors, Shapiro's figurative language forces his readers to struggle to contemplate the difficult nature of description. Because the metaphors are different than the conventional range of associations attached to an object, the reader must question what they think they know and how they know it. While we are used to images reinforcing visual or oral understanding, Shapiro's metaphors move the images into a primarily cognitive space.

Here is an example of metamorphosing metaphors from Shapiro's most recent collection of poetry, *A Burning Interior*: "The Eiffel / was nothing but numbers / like a lecture / by Plato" ("Song of the Eiffel Tower," 21). This image of the Eiffel tower made of numbers is unexpected because it undercuts the tower's romantic connotations and turns the reality of the building into an abstraction. The reader must reimagine the tower as something not made of metal or even myth but of numbers. If Shapiro had ended the metaphor here, the image would be abstract, but it would be abstract the way a Klee painting is abstract—there would still be an image to visualize. The expansion of the metaphor transforms the lines from image to idea. We are forced to see the tower as simultaneously made of numbers and as a lecture by Plato. There is no sensual link between the objects compared, thus forcing Shapiro's metaphors to work cognitively instead of visually or orally. The metaphor reminds the reader how numbers are like Plato's lectures: they both reject the complexity of the world in favor of the idealized version. Math, like Plato's forms, is a means of pure abstraction.

The following metaphor from "The Seasons" functions in a similar way as the one in "Song of the Eiffel Tower": "I saw the ruins of poetry / Of a poetry / Of a parody and it was / Terraces and gardens / A mural bright as candy" (*ALO* 81). The poem forces the reader to question her conventional associations. Most people would think of ruins as dark and dreary, yet Shapiro turns them into a garden, and then to "A mural bright as candy." Each stage of the metaphor's development serves to further remove the subject from its visual or sonic origins. One might think that Shapiro is dismissing description as a mode. However, I would argue that the elements are neither completely random nor ironic. The lines capture the feeling of loss, the particular sadness that comes when fair weather taunts one's inner storms. In this way, they create a new kind of description, one that reflects an awareness of the dangers of thinking in conventional ways.

Shapiro's liturgical repetitions work in a similar way to his mercurial metaphors. In both cases, the poem's structure connects elements from different contexts, allowing Shapiro's particular sort of transforming magic to transpire. It is impossible to open one of his books without finding one of his dazzling prayer-like lists. This list in "To A Swan" in *House (Blown Apart)* is typical in its combining of disparate elements and apparent contradictions:

> Then you were born, swallowing dismissing and rising.
> Then you were born, angry and artful as a blue white swan.
> Then you were born, painting loud appearances.
> Then you were born, in the right place like a thumb and a tongue.
> Then you were born, the animal in detail, impure and good.
> Then you were born, breaking up rain ice and information.
> Then you were born, fanatic nut to crack a riddle.
> Then you were born, nude new and dissimilar.
> Then you were born, in a lake like hidden art.
> Then you were born, like a baked sculpture.
> Then you were born, silent repetitive and good.
> Then you were born, swallowing blue-gray and nude.
> Then you were born, blind as unusual and tempting like a tongue.
> Then you were born, out of fanatic architecture and repeating windows.
> (*HBA* 50)

What connects the disjunctive elements in these lines is sound, alliteration, and slant rhyme. In the first line, each of the gerunds contains "s" sounds; the next line contains two adjectives that start with "a" and the sixth, "tongue" and "thumb." The off-rhyme is subtler, but just as effective in pairs such as "lake" and baked," and "nude" and "good." Like a jazz improviser or an abstract expressionist, Shapiro riffs on the repeating thread, playing with the sounds to keep the reader interested in the refrain. The result is that the meaning of words changes within a single line, or, as Wittengestein might say it, words move from one kind of language game to another. For example, in the line "fanatic nut to crack a riddle," the word combination "fanatic nut" is primarily sonic, then when "to crack" is added, the line becomes a reference to a cliché, then "a riddle" moves the line out of the cliché into a kind of commentary on the line. This sort of wordplay takes place within many of the lines.

To me what is most interesting is how these outrageous lists form their own kind of paradoxically antidescriptive mode of description. "To a Swan" captures what some would call "a mythic oneness"; I would prefer to call it ontological chaos, that moment when objects exist without consciousness' false divisions. The poem does a wonderful job of capturing the moment one feels most alive and creative. The birth of a swan is a metaphor for the feeling that seems impossible to capture in words, yet through his word juggling, Shapiro captures, or perhaps recreates the feeling. By moving words out of their accepted contexts or switching their context mid-line, Shapiro also moves the reader out of her conventional way of thinking. Disjunction becomes a mode of describing what is indescribable, of capturing the way life defeats attempts to limit it.

"After a Lost Original," like much of Shapiro's poetry, contains a dialogue. Often dialogue in Shapiro's poems works as a form of disjunction. Voices speak *at* each other, (instead of *to* each other), echoing each other's lines rather than responding directly. Dialogue becomes a method of changing perspective. In the poem "In Memory of Goofy" in *A Burning Interior,* cartoon characters from different cartoons mourn Goofy's death and discuss questions of art, "perspective," and the grid system. Then Shapiro brings in the voice of his son Daniel. The poem moves from the world of cartoons to the world of flesh, then back again. The poem ends:

> Now Goofy's gone and all his five-act plays
> His stories neatly typed, his wasted too-commercial years.
> He was expert in light. Bad taste, bad taste just thinking,
> Cried Jughead, but most for saying anything, after all.

> Then Daniel in a t-shirt chirped brightly
> I like birds of prey and he liked songbirds
> I like a raptor circling wildly
> He liked a sparrow singing on a mirror.
> But all the flightless birds are howling for a charm.
> And the black window is draped in green for Goofy.
> Return, return, lost student of the plague.
>
> (*BI* 52–53)

Part of what is shocking, and also moving, about this poem is the way it catches the reader off-guard. By bringing in voices in a variety of contexts, Shapiro changes the rules, preventing the reader from becoming complacent. Thus the grief expressed does not become too easy or containable. This is first seen in the lines "bad taste, bad taste," which can be seen as Shapiro's way of speaking through Jughead, to express his horror at his own attempt to memorialize his former student through such ridiculous characters. By bringing in Daniel at the end of the poem, Shapiro shatters the illusion of the poem as being about Goofy's death. In addition to being about grief, the poem becomes a meditation on the absurdity of trying to capture pain in art.

Like many of Shapiro's poems that contain dialogue, "In Memory of Goofy" contains lines that are very direct and straightforward such as "Return, Return, lost student of the plague." Because dialogue is multivoiced and doesn't present a single version of reality, it provides Shapiro with a space for a more transparent use of language compared to his other poems. Often Shapiro uses this space to write in an overtly didactic voice. To me, this tone in Shapiro's poetry is compelling because it is in contrast to the more disjunctive side of his writing.

The dialogue poems that are most overtly didactic often contain a conversation between the old and the young. This is true of all his poetry, not just of the later work. For example, *Poems From Deal*, Shapiro's second collection, published when he was still in college, starts with a conversation between a son and his father. In *To An Idea*, Victor Hugo's petty thief, Jean Valjean, is imagined as a comic older poet, and in "A Burning Interior," Pushkin's angel returns to Earth to give the poem's speaker advice. This form allows Shapiro to admonish without giving up his skeptical approach to language and representation. On an autobiographical level, it might also relate to Shapiro's having been a poetry prodigy; the idea of a young poet's conversation is natural for a writer who spent his teenage years surrounded by older poets and then became a teacher himself.

One of my favorite poems, "House of the Secret" from *After a Lost Original*, is a conversation between an old poet (in this case, "an old dead poet") and a younger, though not young, poet. Like much of Shapiro's work, the poem recasts concerns from his earlier poems. Unlike much of his other poetry, the first two stanzas are relatively direct. It begins:

> I met the old dead poet
> And told him I no longer loved my work
> As I had as a child or even fifteen
> Sorry I had not written someone else's poems but it was
>   already written
>
> He told me, Never think of others or of yourself
> Never do anything for others or for yourself
> And never write poetry for another or for yourself
> Or yourselves.
>
> (ALO 21)

I love these stanzas' slight humor, the way that the idea of the poet as both old and deceased is stated in such a deadpan manner, as well as the way the repetition makes the poet's wise advice sound somewhat absurd. Still, the poem's tone is far from ironic. The old poet's admonition is a useful corrective for a speaker whose ego is too caught up in his work's worth. Even the way the poet describes the self, moving it from a singular to plural, is a useful corrective to the speaker's self-pity.

A poet whose conception of didacticism was more classical might end the poem with the advice. I think of C. P. Cavafy's great poem "The First Step," where the young poet Evmenis complains about his poetic output. The poem ends with Evmenis' mentor Theocritiois telling him how wonderful it is that he has written any poems at all. Instead of ending on the dead poet's guidance, Shapiro's poem, through image and metaphor, explores the consequence of the advice instead of merely accepting it. The language of the poem shifts from the transparent questioning of the first section to the imagistic enactments of the second.

> The camera was hidden under the floor like a boat
> The poem hung from the branch above the silver bridge
> Criticism that does not end, even in Paradise
> We think it is a bridge because it is silver. It is not a bridge.
> Lost is lost.
>
> (*ALO* 21)

This poem ends with images that explore the relationship between reality and description. A camera that is "hidden" and perhaps travels "like a boat" serves as wonderful metaphor for the aesthetic philosophy present in Shapiro's poems. "Camera" connotes clarity; people think of photography as a more objective mode of representation than painting. Shapiro's line reverses this assumption; the camera becomes an icon of subjectivity and murkiness, something unseen and in motion. In contrast, the poem, usually seen as a subjective mode of representation, becomes clear. Still, in both cases, both modes of representation, the poem and the camera, remain out of reach. The poet wishes to retrieve them so he could write the poem as he had written at fifteen, but these poems, like the past, are now unattainable.

As in "In Memory of Goofy," the poem contains a warning against thinking of art as a clear representation of life. The image of the bridge can be viewed as related to issues of representation. The bridge connotes the idea of a connection between "raw experience" and the description of that experience. We might assume that the poem is a bridge between the living and the dead, or between one person's experience and another's, but it is not. Just because a work of art is beautiful (i.e. "silver") does not mean that it can bridge the distances between people, or between experience and representation. In a similar way, the poem about Goofy undercuts its narrative in order to remind the reader how false singular narratives are as a means to describe both grief and the world.

Shapiro's use of disjunctive language and dialogue is related to the recurring theme in his poetry that language and art are copies of originals that no longer exist and might never have existed. This theme is most obvious in the title and the title poem of his eighth collection, *After a Lost Original*:

> When the translation and the original meet
> The doubtful original and the strong mistranslation
> The original feels lost like a triple pun
> And the translation cries, Without me you are lost
> Then be my dream, thin as the definition
> Of a trance in a garden
> The ambiguous friend responds, Perhaps I do astonish you
> Like a boy confused with a butterfly's dream
> But you are my dream now, after all
> If I don't think of you, you disappear
> After which they both comically disappear
> Like a slice through two trees for a thousand years
> Return knowing coldly a need for guerdons, guardians
> Letters written on clouds, snakes on curtains and naked devices
> Frighten them no longer since they live only together
> Father and son refracted through blue green black moss
> They travel together to the margins of a cloud.
>
> (*ALO* 11)

The poem is a reimagining of the Taoist philosopher Chuang Tzu's famous butterfly dream in which the philosopher dreams he is a butterfly dreaming about being a man. The philosopher wonders how he is to know what is reality and what is the dream— is he a man dreaming he is a butterfly or a butterfly dreaming he is a man? In Shapiro's poem, it is language and / or poetry itself that is facing this dilemma. Reality (i.e., the original) is "weak" and the copy of it (i.e., the translation) is strong. By reversing the usual assumption about the relationship between reality and representation, the poem suggests that it is impossible to tell the difference between them. Like Chung Tzu, who wondered if he was a man dreaming he was a butterfly or visa versa, language does not know if it is a mimetic representation of reality or if reality is created by language. By the end of the poem, there is no difference between reality and language. The two are inseparable, working in total unison; they disappear together and travel together in to "margins of cloud," a metaphor for ambiguity. Shapiro calls them "Father and Son," but he doesn't say who is the father or who is the son. By the end of the poem, it has become clear that their relationship is fluid, and it makes no difference who sired whom.

Through its ambiguity, the poem recasts conventional ideas about mimesis. It makes me think of Plato's famous criticism of art as a poor copy of a copy of the ideal (or the forms). In Shapiro's retelling, it is the copy (or the translation) that is powerful, and the original that is weak; the poem thus turns the whole ideal of art as a copy on its ear. Shapiro's poem is not arguing against the idea of representation per se; instead, his poem suggests that the representation is just as much a part of life as the original; the two are one. His poem refutes the conventional way of thinking of representation as something that can be whole, like a map. The problem with the map metaphor for representation is that the world is not static. Reality is changing every minute, and maps are unable to represent change and time. The original will always be lost and weak, because it is so difficult to represent in a mode that does not acknowledge time. This view of art relates to the Shapiro's use of disjunction. Like many other of Shapiro's other poems, "After a Lost Original" suggests that life itself is contradictory and ambiguous. The poems are disjunctive as a means both to mimic and be part of this reality. Like the copy and the original in "After a Lost Original," reality and art are inseparable in the aesthetic philosophy that reveals itself in Shapiro's poetry.

However, Shapiro's poetry does not mystify the limits of language; his poems still try to communicate. Although Shapiro acknowledges the difficulty, he does not relinquish the attempt. Shapiro's elegies and quasidialogues with his friends James Schuyler and Joe Ceravolo are memorable because they show that Shapiro is not too skeptical about representation to address the dead without artifice. In "Voice," he writes to Schuyler "I am amazed by your courage" (*ALO* 69), and in "Weequahic Park in the Dark," he writes to Ceravolo, "Oh Joe full of the dignity of the seasons your school" (*BI* 100). Though the emotions expressed are raw, the context of these lines keeps the poems from becoming sentimental. The elegy to Schuyler is part of a larger seventeen-section poem that begins with a discussion of the danger of turning sentiment into kitsch. This consciousness of such a danger makes his attempt at elegy even more moving. In a similar way, the poem about Ceravolo is concerned with the difficulty of expression. In it he writes:

> You explained—
> I see the words around the emotion
> Then I write them down—
> It was your system of the spider-web
> You were sad
> But couldn't explain

> Missing you now like an oak in 1962
> Or the word oak
> I see your spider-web I write it down
> Open to me, Weequahic Park.
> (*BI* 100–01)

Here Shapiro explains Ceravolo's method of writing poetry and tries it out himself. The lines, "like an oak in 1962 / or the word oak," show the difficulty of creating art out of raw pain. The metaphors appear lousy on purpose. The failed attempt at figurative language demonstrates the limits of trying to create art out of life. (Of course, there's no way an oak in 1962 could miss anyone. In this way, the line shows the futility of personification.) In the next line, he asks the park, a metonym for the time he spent with Ceravolo, to "open" for him. It doesn't. Just as metaphors are futile, so too is the desire to return to the past. The poem works both as an elegy and as a meditation of the limits of elegy. Ultimately, the poem is more of a gesture toward his friend than a monument of him. While most elegies define the person they are about, Shapiro's is more about the difficulty of writing the poem. The poem is didactic by example; it shows Shapiro's love for Ceravolo, but does so delicately. Shapiro does not attempt to define his friend in the poem the way elegies traditionally have; instead, he attempts unsuccessfully to engage his friend in a conversation. This trepidation towards the process of elegy keeps the poem from objectifying or simplifying the emotion.

While Shapiro's dialogues between the old and the young and the living and the dead might clearly show his didactic side, I would say that all of his work can be seen as pedagogical. For Shapiro, concerns about representation and the limits of knowledge become questions that affect not only aesthetics, but also politics and love. These questions affect not only how one should write poetry, but also how one should live life. Shapiro's poetry shows how important it is to acknowledge the limits of what we can know and describe so that we can avoid objectifying it, so we can avoid projecting our own desires onto others and believing it is the other, not ourselves, we see.

Shapiro's love poems are very conscious of the difficulty of describing another person. They also display an awareness of the history of love poetry as a mode of idealization and objectification. He cries of "a bloody misogyny" (*ALO* 55) in one poem after a fragmented image of a woman. In another he asks, "to whom does the you in your poem / Refer" (*ALO* 33). That poem's answer is to avoid this impossible question. One of his most humorous poems, "Dante and Beatrice (at Forty-Seven)," is a meditation on a pair of gold bronze sculptures of the literary lovers. As the poem progresses, Beatrice transforms from the idealized version in the *Divine Comedy* into a "gift from Mickey Mouse" to "Goofy," then to an image of a modern woman "working for better schools for / black children in South Africa / and justice like a child's story" whom the speaker urges to "sleep with Romeo / Marat" (*BI* 25–26). The shifting of Beatrice's image suggests the absurdity of romantic idealization. The poem ends, "God is a candle" (*BI* 26), an image that suggests how little we are able to see of each other. The other is, of course, only available to us in fragments because the source of knowledge ("God") is delicate and flickering.

This concern with epistemology and questions of representation also informs the way in which Shapiro's poetry is political. In the epigram for the section of "Voice" called "the Uncertainty," Shapiro ironically quotes Henry Kissinger: "There are no awards for showing / your uncertainty in foreign policy" (*ALO* 68). Kissinger is clearly the villain here. Because of his refusal to admit his own uncertainty, he escalated misguided wars and encouraged war crimes. The poem's demonstration of the poet's own uncertainty becomes a counter to Kissinger's arrogance. In "Song for Hannah Arendt," Shapiro writes, "out of the essential mistranslation / emerges an illegitimate nation" (*BI* 15). The poem suggests that how we represent or translate our experience into words affects politics on the deepest level.

Occasionally in Shapiro's work the connection between ethics and his skepticism about conventional ideas of representation and knowledge is addressed directly. Shapiro's reworking of his poem "The Lost Golf Ball," "A Found Golf Ball," explores this issue:

> Part of the universe has been found. But only part!
> but it is the light of dead stars
> if it shall console you
> and the light of our own dying sun
> and it is the light of dark matter
> along the edges of our time like the exhausted flesh of a single flower
> though it could be "something else," normal and glowing
> like your mother's voice . . .
> and my father's name

> which bore no middle initial
> so he gave me a middle initial
> so I would not write in time of war
> No Middle Initial
> Part of the Universe had been found Only a part!
>
> (*BI* 42)

Here the metaphor of the lost original in the earlier poems is translated into the language of astronomy. Instead of an "original" and a translation, Shapiro gives us the idea of dying stars and the image of stars we see in the sky. Because the stars are so far away and light takes so long to travel across space, the stars we see lighting the sky may very well be dead by the time we see them. This metaphor is analogous to the idea of representation that repeats throughout his poetry. In other words, by the time we represent something, what we are representing may have already changed or ceased to exist. The poem suggests that vision works in a similar way to representation. We cannot know if what we perceive or what we represent is the same as reality.

What I find moving about the poem is the way it takes this epistemological concern and makes it intimate. Instead of being nihilistic about our limits, Shapiro embraces them and tries to show the reader their beauty and use. We may not be able to embrace the actual stars, but their after-effects (the light) should still be able to console us. He compares the fragments of the universe to a "mother's voice," and "a father's name." Just as we cannot know the stars, we cannot know our parents in their completeness. We can only experience parts of them, a mother's voice, which did not sound like what we hoped for, or a middle initial, which the father just made up because he didn't have one. Still, Shapiro is not suggesting that we should be angry about the delicacy of these fragments. He repeats the line "Part of the Universe has been found." The tone here sounds revelatory and prayer-like; it is a call to embrace what we can. The poem even ends with a reference to prayer. Shapiro writes, "It is not our custom to pray in the direction of the Tower of Babel / And it's all ordinary, the stars, the stuff of love, and the dark found universe" (*BI* 42). He seems to be suggesting that it might be a mistake *not* to pray in the "direction of the Tower of Babel." Perhaps if we acted in a way that was more reverential toward what the story of the Tower demonstrated to be the limits of language, we would be better people, less likely to be arrogant about "the stuff of love."

Shapiro's poetry can be seen as a sort of prayer in the direction of Babel. The poems' indeterminate surfaces and shifting perspectives show the difficulty of communication, but also the importance of the attempt. They show how challenging it is to know the world and to represent it, but they are never fatalistic about this difficulty; they never mystify language or surrender the attempt to use it. His poems show how slippery language can be, but they are never just about words. They never relinquish the desire to represent and communicate. This struggle to communicate despite the obstacles, along with the corresponding desire to be honest about acknowledging one's limits, is at the heart of Shapiro's didactic approach. Because he is able to demonstrate these ideas, as opposed to stating them, the poems become more than doctrines; they are models of how to live.

David Shapiro:
New Jersey as Trope

Carole Stone

GIVEN THAT DAVID SHAPIRO PURPOSEFULLY ESCHEWS BIOGRAPHY IN his poetry, the title of my essay may appear fictional. Shapiro was born in Newark, New Jersey in 1947 and grew up nearby, in the affluent suburb of Millburn. Shapiro, in spite of his antagonism to biographical references, does, in fact, tell the reader about his origins. For example, he explicitly states, "Since I was born in the city of Newark" (*TI* 63). Furthermore, the title of his second book of poetry, *Poems from Deal*, written in 1969, refers to the New Jersey upper middle class seaside resort of Deal where the poet and his family lived when he was a child. As a native of New Jersey, Shapiro is in good company with poets such as Allen Ginsberg and William Carlos Williams, each of whom lived in a town (Passaic and Rutherford respectively) not far from Millburn. His decision to seek mentors who were poets from the New York School—O'Hara, Koch, and Ashbery —was more a rejection of confessional poetry than of his New Jersey roots. Moreover, he rejected not only confessionalism, but regionalism, choosing Manhattan's iconography over New Jersey's. And what young poet would not? New Jersey smacks of provincialism, malls, the turnpike, Garden State Parkway, suburbia—not very inspiring for a young poet.

And yet, references to the state where he was born inhabit his work like a shadow self. New Jersey as trope allows Shapiro to return to a familiar structure that is both personal and poetic. Known primarily for his experimentation, beneath his surreal imagery and collage, Shapiro uses New Jersey imagery as a counter-force, which also provides him with a means of writing about family history without being explicitly autobiographical. For example, Shapiro's elegies for his mother, who died in 1975, can be compared to Allen Ginsberg's *Kaddish* in its New Jersey setting. So, too, as with Ginsberg, this locale is a vehicle for addressing the father-son relationship. For example, he defines his father, as a Millburn doctor the way Allen Ginsberg defined his father as a Passaic school teacher. *Kaddish* can also be viewed as relative to Shapiro's Jewish roots. *Lateness*, written in 1977, and dedicated "To My Father and in Memory of My Mother," contains enough elegies to be viewed as a prayer for the dead. The poet's identity is at stake here and, as with all of us, whether we reject or accept our beginnings, they matter. My purpose is not to hunt for referential content in images of New Jersey but to show how they represent (if one can use this word about Shapiro's mostly surreal work) where he came from, who he is, and where he went as a mature poet.

My thesis is that buried beneath experimentation, disjunction, and willful rejection of biography, Shapiro uses his origins as an emotional mooring to family and to the representational poetic credo he turned his back on. In Shapiro's work, though buried beneath linguistic uncertainty and verbal wildness, geography equals representation. In this sense, William Carlos Williams, especially in *Paterson*, can be seen as having had as much influence on Shapiro as John Ashbery and Frank O'Hara had in their cityscapes.

While Shapiro himself sees *Paterson* as containing elements of "rootedness within a city which is a world,"[1] recognizing that Williams's collage technique is more reality centered than his is, I believe the Jersey world of Deal is concrete enough to emerge clearly from Shapiro's abstractions. I cite Williams and Ginsberg also because their two New Jersey centered epics, *Paterson* and *Kaddish*, are a form Shapiro says he always wished he could write. Instead he writes sequences but said, "I really do regard my sequences as a long poem."[2] I would therefore argue that New Jersey and its poets have enabled Shapiro to write the long poems he wants to write.

Thomas Fink observes that "From the mid-1960s to the mid-1970s, David Shapiro followed Ashbery's lead by pursuing experiments with language as a dominantly non-referential or even *anti*referential medium."[3] And yet, somehow, in some poems, in some way, the referential intrudes with New Jersey as a trope. To quote Fink again, "While the text never emerges as 'readable' in a traditional sense, it is always hovering near the threshold of readability."[4] Shapiro acknowledges that he is more personal and understandable than critics recognize: "I am not a confessional poet, but there's enough in me of Jewish guilt to make a lot of my poems more naturalistic than what other people might find."[5]

In this chapter I will focus primarily on *Poems from Deal*, because this book most explicitly refers to New Jersey, especially in the long poem about Deal, and owes a debt to Williams and Ginsberg, but also to Wallace Stevens, another practitioner of the long poem to which Shapiro aspires. More importantly, Stevens's wit and playful language influenced Shapiro. For example, consider the double entendre of the word "deal." I think of the title of Stevens's poem "The Emperor of Ice-Cream." Ice cream is one of the most touted foods at the seaside. While ice cream is all-American, in the context of "Poems from Deal" there is a particular seascape implied. Additionally, Stevens's line "take from the dresser of deal,"[6] suggests Shapiro is making a deal with Stevens that he will keep his personal references obscure, use figurative language, and be abstract as Stevens was. And "deal" is a synonym for pine or fir cut to standard sizes, a plain wood. Shapiro, is also signaling that a solid reality, namely the deal he was dealt in New Jersey, will not be obliterated from his aesthetic. As Carl Whithaus points out, "Shapiro constantly makes the reader aware that language is trying to provide access to someone's memories, to the past."[7]

In the first poem, "Ode," in *Poems from Deal*, Shapiro, in a command to the reader and himself, orders, "Identify the note in your head" (13). The geography of the poem suggests the Jersey shore with its "Atlantic northeastern" and the densely populated state's traffic—"though traffic gets mixed up here." The fact that this is an authoritarian order is stated in the line "Clear and parental caveat," and the following one, "Oh doctor is this your advice?" Shapiro's father, a doctor, is invoked and then as if to say, so what does his advice matter, "He went away on a Public Service Bus." The Public Service image is a direct reference to the New Jersey Public Service Transportation Company. More importantly, as a doctor, Shapiro's father devoted himself to public service. There is a suggestion of neglect in this double entendre. For it is the father who goes away on public transportation "into a suitable cave of his choice," invoking Plato's cave, as he is "Also contending for the child artist." Buses, being the preteen means of transportation is why Shapiro states, "And a teenager turns into a car." The poem is a struggle for the child's artistic soul as in the lines: "My mother woke from a nap / She didn't even bother to put on a slip, / She bent her eyes and gave me a toy / A mother gives a delirious boy," the maternal and erotic attempt to seduce the son into an artistic vocation. There is a suggestion of Marc Chagall's incongruity and the violins that abound in his paintings: "Like a cake that moves in the sky. / Now out of boyhood I tune up the violin / Neither low nor high, her only son." Shapiro, who was a violin prodigy at the age of five, uses these veiled autobiographical references with their Jersey iconography in the first poem of the book, aptly called "Ode," to establish family and locale as the origins of his artistic identity. Like Keats in his odes, the young poet is struggling with his relation to poetry and to his family.

Allusions to Newark that invoke the theme of discovering his poetic identity continue in the book's third poem "In Memory of Your Body." Shapiro's speaker, who may or may not be the poet, says in the first section of seven, "I took an early disappointment to heart, / And remain a bachelor at seventy-two" (*PFD* 15), a fictional exaggeration that echoes Stevie Smith's uncanny poem "I Remember" with its opening lines of "It was my bridal night I remember, / An old man of seventy-three."[8] This unexpected English association with its weird eroticism reverses itself with a concrete reference to Newark's Weequahic Park in section two: "My father would wake me up / And walk me around Weequahic Park / And the sometimes turbulent Weequahic Lake" (*PFD* 15). The poem moves closer to Wordsworth's musings on his development as a poet in "Lines Composed Above Tintern Abbey." Shapiro's debt to the English poets, contemporary as well as Romantic, adds to the disjunctive quality of his verse because their influence coexists among so many unrelated images from varied cultures. His graduate study at Cambridge University no doubt contributed to his English resources. A specific locale, England, contributes to the specific locale of Newark. Weequahic Park is Newark's Tintern Abbey.

In sections two and three of this seven section poem, we see the poet growing up, seeking a vocation and an artistic identity and rebelling against his family and teachers:

> I escaped the attention of my teachers,
> Who were more interested in money

> But who respected me among the books.
> They destined me to be a
> Doctor! A violinist or a professor.
> If they had discovered and analyzed
> My waking dreams, however,
> They would have formed other conclusions.
>
> When I was sixteen, disgusted
> With everything except their abstractions
> I qualified as a virtuoso
> But my bow was (speedily) flung away.
>   (*PFD* 15)

The speaker may or may not be Shapiro but the autobiographical references are clear enough for me to see the poem as an *Ars Poetica* in which the poet bids farewell to New Jersey to become a New York poet. In the final section with a title, "And Now a Final Toast," there is enough braggadocio and celebration in the cadences to add another poet with Jersey roots and long poems to Shapiro's influences, namely Walt Whitman:

> To great feats of harmony.
> To the dream of youth, and the harvest of tragedy!
> To inarticulate sounds—they could carry no further.
> To the enviable islands.
> To splendid convulsions, and a crisis in American history.
> To a freak of taste.
> To that vast eclipse we undergo.
> To the slightest emotions.
> To the spot which, it seems, is not far distant.
> To interchange.
> To empty, indefatigable fluency. To New York!
> To interchange of gifts.
>   (*PFD* 17)

In this last section, the poet of the senses (New York) overpowers the poet of naturalism (New Jersey) of the earlier sections.

But Shapiro has not left Deal behind. "Poems from Deal," the title poem of the volume, continues the argument the poet is having with himself over identity, as the speaker appears to be carrying on the conversation with his alter-ego by addressing a "you." The references and language are less accessible, like a stream of consciousness, as the speaker merges one unfamiliar image with another. Here are a few examples: "The horse stamps / across the beach: a passive part" (*PFD* 24). And, "She said nothing slipping inside the streak except / One day you will accept the land of rectangles." These dissonant images could all be explained by the first line of the poem, "How wonderful to be in the arms of cerebral creatures." Where the poet lives now is in his mind but even there, particulars of Deal invade his unconscious. "I spoke to Uncle Louie of Deal Bridge. / He said I could pass like the dead, very merry" (*PFD* 25). Just the mention of an Uncle Louie conjures up a Jewish family history. Significantly, the uncle is guarding the gates to Deal, or Hell, where he guards it like Cerberus, allowing his nephew to pass into the land of the dead. Who will he find there? It appears that the you who the speaker addresses doesn't love him, as embodied in "my pants and shoes that are curtains / cleats of desire; crease / that destroyed the bulwarks at Deal." The poem becomes more discordant with imagery of Arizona, fascism, Napoleon, the United Nations scatter shot in the final sections. What remains solid is the Jersey shore and Deal: water images abound throughout the poem. "fresh water," hot shower," "wet page," "it rained in Switzerland," "lightening storm," "waterfall." "'For every sandpiper there's a giant dirigible sound.' / 'Never better' Never together' / 'They dragged physique out of the Atlantic." The speaker asks:

> Why do we invent communities
> in the clouds? Their strictures against children
> posted in the castles at Deal:
> WALK ON THE MATTRESSES; DON'T WAKE THE BABIES.
> (*PFD* 26)

So Deal is a community that pays no attention to its dreamers for whom it posts rules on structures I take to be beach sandcastles, as the homes in Deal are castles. As one who has been restricted by Deal, the speaker accuses the "you" who taught him "prose monodies" and "spelling stories," thus, educating him in useless facts, of emotional neglect. "You didn't appear to be there" (*PFD* 27). Ultimately this is a poem about loss. As Carl Whithaus observes, "One rebels successfully against authority (parental, societal) and then one wonders, did I really need to do that? Doubt and anxiety return. To abandon an early talent, to abandon what parents desire for you, say as in Shapiro's case, to abandon music for poetry is a haunting choice." Numerous references to the loss of music resonate throughout the volume, a central one: "Probably three-quarters of yourself remains lividly attached to a musical instrument at home" (*PFD* 39). If Deal was music and "you give away your violin" (*PFD* 52), as the speaker notes in "Elegy to Sports," then the sense of loss that pervades the book is loss of home. Therefore, as Shapiro commands in "To My Dead Son," "All roads to Deal have dried up, return to your wings" (*PFD* 32). Who the dead son is remains unclear, but certainly he might be the poet speaker who has died as a musician and must return to Pegasus's wings, poetry.

Poems from Deal begins with a poem titled "Ode" and surreally ends with another called "Ode," completing the speaker's journey from New Jersey to New York. References in the poem to painters, to a Frank who is undoubtedly his friend, Frank O'Hara, show that the musical prodigy from Newark has moved on to the art and poetry world of Manhattan. The speaker says "I have something of New York in me" (PFD 59). Fittingly the poem is in couplets, suggesting a more contained world of craft and precision. The poem has none of the wild abandon and hysteria of the earlier poems, "In Memory of Your Body" and "Poems from Deal." The poet possesses a tighter control over language and the formal structure provides a more rational closure to the volume.

The obscure speaker is still giving orders, though more politely and gently as in the opening lines: "Permit me to take this sleeping man? And I will help him on his way" (*PFD* 59). Deal and adolescence are gone. "The poem must leap over the cut-offs," is a wonderful line that both says goodbye to youth and looks forward to a life of poetry. In the final "Ode," the voice of the mature poet emerges. I detect an homage to Keats who died too young to fully mature as a poet, but whose letters became an avatar of poetic truth.

In later books, Shapiro's overt references to his beginnings are more general; but they exist. For example, in *After a Lost Original*, in "House" his description takes him back to his origins. "In the beginning was the house / A nice sofa, inveterate tuba, and the impossible / flow of music" (*ALO* 46). The Biblical opening both universalizes and concretizes Shapiro's Jewish suburban background as does "Television was the little house / full of games and giveaways and human / sacrifice / It was too coherent, too many tears, too / much winglessness / Songlessness." This is a house without poetry; yet it raised a poet.

I'd like to end this discussion of New Jersey in Shapiro's work with "The Destruction of the Bulwarks at Deal" from *A Man Holding An Acoustic Panel* (1971). "Bulwarks at Deal" appeared previously in the poem, "Poems from Deal," and these words forefront section one. They echo Williams's "Tract" in which he castigates his townspeople for their showiness in a funeral procession. The opening lines, "To begin with, my rising with you near the Deal apartments; / and my heart always in ferocious projects, worries you / with distances and dark, with the perishing tendrils" (*MHAP* 44), suggest ruin (the projects) and the involvement of the speaker with his own preoccupations, a play on the word projects. The notion of ruin embodied in "How many, our truest summers gone, the townsmen plundered you," in Shapiro's lack of nostalgia for the lost summers of youth is seen in the line, "while the bloated gulls beat past the poles"; the poles may be telephone poles or street light poles or even ocean poles, all of which suggest what Deal has become to the poet. Yet Deal remains "in your hands still of the absurd, individual gift," that the poet retains, inspiration, as he recognizes in the following lines that Deal as the muse causes suffering and will, if delved into too deeply, disappear:

> But if I tried to grab the child, this moment he becomes me
> Or to seize you without suffering
> my eyes in their skinny gaze hold, cover you no more.
> (*MHAP* 44)

In "Long Live the Snowflake," a poem from Shapiro's later work, *A Burning Interior*, he writes:

> Long live the catachresis
> of our lives in New Jersey
> and Troy and in wandering eraser fluid
> and books of many naked devices.
> (*BI* 13)

New Jersey is a "catachresis," which means a deliberately paradoxical figure of speech. Thus it is a paradox to grow up in New Jersey and become a poet of surrealism and experimentation. But by praising "our lives in New Jersey," which are ordinary, he asserts that the notion of becoming a poet in New Jersey is as real as becoming one in classical Greece. As Homer, the Greek poet, created a hero who wandered the seas, Shapiro's speaker wanders in "eraser fluid and books." What are the "naked devices?" This image is obscure. As always, David Shapiro, a master of figurative language, manages to incorporate enough mystery among concrete biographical references to leave the reader uncomfortable, but engaged.

Notes

1. Shapiro, *John Ashbery: An Introduction to the Poetry* (New York: Columbia University Press, 1979), 70.
2. Joanna Fuhrman, "Pluralist Music: An Interview with David Shapiro," *Rain Taxi Online* (Fall 2002) *http://www.raintaxi.com/online/2002/fall/shapiro.shtml*.
3. Thomas Fink, *The Poetry of David Shapiro* (Rutherford, NJ: Fairleigh Dickinson Press, 1993), 38.
4. Ibid., 41.
5. Joanna Fuhrman, "Pluralistic Music: An Interview with David Shapiro."
6. Wallace Stevens, *The Collected Poems* (New York: Knopf, 1977), 64.
7. Carl Whithaus, "Immediate Memories: (Nostalgic) Time and (Immediate) Loss in the Poetry of David Shapiro," Rocky Mountain Modern Language Association (1997) http://rmmla.wsu.edu/ereview/53.1/articles/Whithaus/asp.
8. Stevie Smith, *Collected Poems* (New York: Oxford University Press, 1976), 33.

David Shapiro and Jasper Johns: Ego in the Egoless Pie

Stephen Paul Miller

DAVID SHAPIRO BELONGS TO THE SECOND GENERATION OF NEW YORK poets arguably to be stimulated more by the visual art of its time than by its literature. Put a bit differently, a receptivity to contemporaneous arts other than literature and poetry directed their poetic influences. For instance, one might argue that, considering the generation prior to Shapiro's, Ashbery may have been influenced by Wallace Stevens through a "lens" of Jackson Pollock.

John Ashbery, James Schuyler, Barbara Guest, Edwin Denby, Kenward Elmslie, and other poets associated with them constitute the first generation of "art-inspired" poets, in part because of their friendships with and immersions in the work and impetuses of painters like Jackson Pollock, Willem de Kooning, Helen Frankenthaler, Joan Mitchell, Grace Hartigan, Larry Rivers, Michael Goldberg, and others within the orbit of Abstract Expressionism or working in response to it. Frank O'Hara, typical of the poets Shapiro emulated, maintained that he and his friends had no sympathetic elder poets to emulate and found greater receptivity and inspiration from New York artists, whom the poets admired, reviewed, catalogued, and curated. In his memoir of Larry Rivers, O'Hara wrote that in the fifties, "the painters were the only generous audience" for him and his poet-friends, then "in [their] early twenties."[1]

According to Edwin Denby, the term "The New York School of Poetry," originally a tongue-in-cheek allusion to the already semi-whimsical name "The New York School of Painting," was "adopted" by the poets "out of homage to the people who had de-provincialized American painting"—the artists "who went to the Cedar" Bar and "had more or less coined the term 'New York School' in opposition to the

School of Paris."[2] "New York subject matter was not the point, "but just as Paris broke through in opposition to, say, the School of Florence, New York was where it was happening and it was these people living in New York who said, 'That's what we want to do.'"

At the beginning of the twenty-first century, John Ashbery is often considered apart from New York School poetry, and New York School poetry in itself is often doubted as a useful concept. However, this affinity to other arts caused New York School poets to consider language as a medium to be cherished and distinguished from what it represents. Even in the cases of the most understandable poems by Schuyler, Koch, and O'Hara, linguistic components such as description (Schuyler), discourse (Koch), and lyrical intensity and hyperbole (O'Hara) become at least as much the subjects of these poems as their referential subjects, which of course also participate in the self-referential linguistic acts that these poems are. In any case, one can imagine Roman Jacobsen making a compelling case for such readings. Certainly, Ashbery's poems are important due at least in some part to the power they give language to generate content.

In terms of American poetry, many poets were influenced by artists. However, New York School poetry is unique for its identification of poetry and language as something somehow on the same "platform" as the other arts and not merely like them, as for instance the critical remarks of Ezra Pound, William Carlos Williams, and Wallace Stevens imply. One might say that there is a movement from early twentieth century identification of poetry with art to mid-century merging of poetry and art to late century investigation of language as a unique medium that runs parallel to the other arts. In this regard, this chapter argues that David Shapiro is a critically essential bridge between New York School and Language poets. Shapiro plays the instrument of language in such a way so as to emphasize both language and instrumentality. One might say that this poet's "open-hooded" forms of sharp linguistic phrasing are instrumental to Shapiro's poems and an understanding of contemporary poetry alike. Shapiro's poetry, one senses, is passionately focused on creating language that is primarily about an oddly possible kind of language as a possibility, an effusive language that welcomes the devices at its disposal yet does not use them to the detriment of linguistic power and possibility in themselves.

Leo Steinberg's analysis of how art became increasingly "horizontal" rather than "vertical" is germane to Shapiro's poetic accomplishment in relation to New York School poetry and painting. Since the Renaissance, the traditional picture plane is seen as a "worldspace ... in correspondence with the erect human posture. The top ... corresponds to where we hold our heads aloft," whereas the "lower edge gravitates to where we place our feet."[3] Even in Abstract Expressionism, this picture plane "affirms verticality as its essential condition," thus suggesting that the Abstract Expressionists were still nature painters. For example, "Pollock's drip paintings cannot escape being read as thickets; Louis' *Veils* mimic natural gravitational force." For Steinberg, around 1950, in Rauschenberg and Dubuffet's art emerged "pictures" that "no longer stimulate vertical fields, but opaque flatbed horizontals," even if the works can be hung. Steinberg's term, "the flatbed picture plane," "borrowed ... from the flatbed printing process," is intended to describe work that alludes symbolically "to hard surfaces such as tabletops, studio floors, charts, bulletin boards—any receptor surface on which objects are scattered, on which data is entered, on which information may be received, printed, impressed—whether coherently or in confusion." In this "radically new orientation, ... the painted surface is no longer the analogue of a visual experience of nature but of operational processes."

Since we tend to equate normal vision with "up" and "down," as we live in a world of gravitational forces, it seemed right to Steinberg to term this old orientation of painting as "vertical." "Horizontal" painting, no longer a model of our perception of the physical world, patterns itself after our thought processes, including the apprehension of nature, culture, and individual subjectivity. Steinberg singles out Rauschenberg's 1949 *White Painting with Numbers* "with its cryptic meander of lines and numbers" as "a work surface that cannot be construed into anything else. Up and down are as subtly confounded as positive-negative space or figure-ground differential. You cannot read it as masonary, nor as system of chains or quoins, and the written ciphers read every way."[4]

The "meander of lines and numbers" is "cryptic" because it seems both coherent and meaningless. The lines create a well-regulated interlocking pattern of columns of rectangles with one end open. This ingenious design occupies our imagination. Purposeless numbers and words—often upside down—emphasize an all-encompassing pointlessness. The importance of pattern, sign, and word as visual and psychological organizing methods was pursued in later years much more vigorously by Jasper Johns than by Rauschenberg.

At least five years before Johns had found his style, Rauschenberg was creating pieces representative of his life's work. Since the two were close friends and eventually roommates when Johns began to do the kind of painting he is now known for, Johns cannot be considered the same kind of pioneer Rauschenberg was. Like David Shapiro, Johns was an early exponent of a distinctively new movement, yet both already had models. Both Johns and Shapiro moved further in the light of these movements, refining precursors' accomplishments to be purer examples of these attainments. However, whereas Shapiro's work amalgamizes diverse styles of first generation New York school poets, Johns had only one nearly contemporary painter to emulate.[5]

At first making small constructions of metal and wood, as Rauschenberg had, Johns, in 1954, destroyed all the work in his possession.[6] Determined to "do only what [he] meant to do, and not what others did," he "tried to remove" traces of others' attainments, so that his "work became a constant negation of impulses."[7] David Shapiro, too, confronted the specter of elders. In 1978, Harold Bloom maintains that Shapiro was still working his way through Ashbery's influence and had yet to make a unique contribution.[8] However, I argue here that Shapiro, surpassing O'Hara, Koch, and Ashbery's influences, creates a new poetry corresponding to the uniqueness of Johns's painting.

Upon meeting O'Hara, Shapiro was most impressed by the seriousness with which he regarded poetry and how hard he worked at it.[9] Poems like "Adieu to Norman, Bonjour to Joan and Jean-Paul,"[10] made O'Hara seem self-indulgent, uncritically accepting of his own work (which he seemed to do quickly), and hopelessly involved with his personal references and friends. However, O'Hara suggests that life is made up of these personal allusions and their acceptance is necessary to affirm life, which he seeks to do in the poem. Shapiro, adopting O'Hara's use of personal associations but deleting from them all hint of what they refer to, creates a purer strain of "horizontal poetry" because the poems and processes of writing them are emphasized over anything the poetry describes. Note these stanzas from Shapiro's long 1977 poem, "The Devil's Trill Sonata":

> And as we entered the Bogey Man
> Edged forward with underwater spearguns
> And so the sweet green violet
> Was permanently closed

We were natives of Alps
And had the power of reducing all cancerous growth
I played you my resonant box of peculiar strings
four open notes.

Unknown woman, unknown physician, unknown Roman
Cut in two by spring vacation
Unknown man, so-called, beside me is a tiny coupon
Eaton's Berkshire Typewriter Paper A 201 and liquid eraser fluid:

Shake well, touch
Blow for instant dry
Retype. Product penetrates.
The rose of the poet and the rose of the botanist are one!

(*L*)

Like Kenneth Koch, Shapiro often repeats a word or phrase in each line of a poem. Whereas Koch tends to use the repeated word at the beginning of each line, taking off from it to achieve odd, improvisatory effects, and O'Hara employs the technique to embellish a point or observation, Shapiro plays with the phrase or word itself, adding a different inflection to it each time so as to emphasize the word itself rather than any point he is making with its use. Consider "An Afternoon with a Lion":

> Towards the lion and up to the lion
> First you were too dazed to gaze into the lion,
> Around the lion and with the lion.
>
> Hand over hand you were getting into the lion,
> Sniffing palm trees and floating upon the lion
> Towards the lion and up to the lion.
>
> In the seventh frame you slipped above the lion
> Into the white sky beyond each lion,
> Around the lion and with the lion.
>
> Now under the lion, smiling under the lion
> It's a light green day edges toward the lion,
> Towards the lion and up to the lion.
>
> But how is one to get out of the lion,
> One's hat and stick sticking out of the lion,
> Around the lion and with the lion?

> You ran away from the lion and away from the lion—
> Amazed and apart, days away from the lion
> Towards the lion and up to the lion,
> Around the lion and with the lion.
>
> (*L*)

Shapiro diverges from Ashbery in much the same way that the Second Generation New York School painters differ from the first. Steinberg observes that the abstractionist Pollock, unlike Johns and Rauschenberg, was still concerned with aesthetic matters related to factors such as "up and down," indicative of the physical world as we know it. (The latter painters may have been concerned with verticality for the sake of reading a symbol, word, or pattern.) Similarly, although Ashbery's poetry may seem abstract, it resembles "normal" narrative because of the presence of a speaker, even if this speaker is unnamed. In his poetic surface, Shapiro either avoids a narrator and subject matter or collages them out of all possibility of continuity, as in "The Mudguard Stroke":

> Perfect bliss (atomized) like a milk drop
> builds a bridge over the valley—too low
> or below the belt—
> the floods of tears like lashing wine grovels by
>   and is gone.
> Under the scaffold bedstead of engraved beech
>   where night gets off the subject
> Barbed wire, trials and tribulations, blackberry and ivy
> The sun hooked up
> In creases and dog-ears and undulations
> from a breast-high sound barrier of stone
> Oh woman in my doorway, in the Straits of Dover
>   with your seven-league boots and key money
>   crawling on apace with a
>   faithful number.
>
> (*PT* 31)

When Rauschenberg erased a de Kooning drawing and exhibited it, Steinberg believes that he transformed it from a vertical to a horizontal work of art, "tilting de Kooning's evocation of a worldspace into a thing produced by pressing down on a desk."[11] Similarly, Shapiro has reworked and omitted and metaphorically "erased" the Ashberian narrator and subject matter from his own work.

A "horizontal poem" needs to eschew normal laws and expectations of everyday logic; John Cage has articulated the purpose of this purposelessness. In the 1930s, Cage came to believe that pitch was too dominant an element in music, since harmony and melody are only determined by pitch. If music was to create a true image of the full spectrum of sound, silence would be a starting point. Therefore, he wished to create a musical composition which could accommodate silence. Duration alone (notation of music in terms of simple, clocked time) could easily record silence.[12] Cage wanted to let sounds "be themselves"—sound as they do without being blurred by harmonic relationships the composer placed each sound within,[13] as he focused on clocked time segments. Cage said, "A single sound by itself is neither musical nor not musical. It is simply a sound" that "can become musical by taking its place in a piece of music,"[14] as can silence. Cage would also wish language "to be itself" in the same way—to be independent of context, since literal meaning has been too dominant, like pitch in music. His procedure of reducing works by Thoreau, Joyce, and others into words and phonemes does not eliminate meaning altogether but forms texts in which such meanings are unintentional.

For Cage, influenced by Zen, music's function is "to sober [sic] and quiet the mind, thus rendering it susceptible to divine influences."[15] Divinity, he felt, was everywhere, and so music's function was to make the complexity and beauty of life in all its forms apparent to listeners. Art should "imitate nature in her manner of operation" as opposed to how nature appeared.[16] Cage wanted "sounds people hear in a concert" to "make them more aware of the sounds they hear in the street, or out in the country, or anywhere they may be."[17] Realizing that absolute silence was impossible, even in a Harvard University chamber designed to exclude all noise, where he could hear his nervous system and blood pressure, Cage redefined silence as unintentional sounds.

In this sense, Shapiro also produces "silent language," although he does not analyze language into its physical components (words and phonemes) but writes a more synthetic poetry of "unintent." Ideas and images are allowed to enter, phrases and sentences are intact, but it is unclear who or if anyone—is speaking and feeling them, as in "An Exercise in Futility":

> . . . three other countries rolled up beside him;
> And on the other side of him, a picture of him
> Where he begs, student-wise, another sage
> For another scheme, like a part of the bending tree
> Of desire. The beaks surround him
> Surround us and lunge out of us like a wish.
>
> Snowflakes bewildered the upper edge of things.
> The bridge is not an argument,
> Nor is it a bridge, in a sense.
> The birds are flying buttresses.
> No impedimenta on the bridge;
> No traveler on the boardwalk; two hands are folded above the tree.
>
> (*TI* 17–18)

"The (horizontal) flatbed picture plane lends itself to any content that does not evoke a prior optical event," says Steinberg.[18] As Cage wishes for his musical compositions, Shapiro's poem makes its audience see (or hear) experience for the first time. A clause such as "The bridge is not an argument" does not evoke any normal kind of prior linguistic event. Horizontal art may utilize representational images but when it does, says Steinberg, it is "conceived as an image of an image. It's a conception which guarantees that the presentation will not be directly that of a worldspace, and that it will nevertheless admit any experience as the matter of representation."[19] For Cage, evoking "worldspace" is inadvisable as it involves the audience in the appearance of nature instead of nature's "manner of operation," and Steinberg's notion of the primacy of "operational processes" in recent painting is congruent with this perspective.

Cage felt that an art which could be produced independently of the artist's intent would not obscure nature's manner of operation, but reveal it. Since one's intentions and desires become involved in everything one does, a means must be found to exclude it from the making of art. One of Cage's first methods of doing this was to place transparent musical notation paper upon a chart of stars in our galaxy. Wherever a star could be seen through the transparent paper, he derived a note through the random means of throwing coins and consulting the *I Ching* for hexagram numbers which in turn denoted a decision concerning the note's silence or sonar existence and pitch.

Jasper Johns, who like David Shapiro, and Cage—a major influence upon both the poet and painter—is an artist of unintention. In 1954, after he destroyed all his previous work in his possession, his next painting, in 1955, utilizes charts, as Cage had done, in order to achieve unintention. Johns paints an American flag. However, unlike Cage's use of charts, Johns's American flag is apparent in the finished product. Johns assures an unintentionality by simply reproducing a predetermined pattern and symbol. Johns's *Flag* represents a dramatically different approach to painting than Rauschenberg's. Whereas Rauschenberg collects and incorporates contemporary images and objects into his work, at times thinking of himself as a "reporter" within the visual arts, Johns paints an image which (with the exception of the stars) has been in existence since the American Revolution. It is also important to note that Johns was predominantly hand painting his images with materials recognizable as an artist's, while Rauschenberg was increasingly collaging "found" or preexisting objects and silk-screening photographs onto his canvases. As I soon show, Shapiro shares Johns's propensity to redo found materials (or words) with means that are characteristic of an artist (or poet).

By painting the American flag, Johns sidesteps the issue of abstraction and representation. In one sense a painting of an American flag *is* an American flag. When painting a symbol, one does not represent or abstract it but rather makes it. A painting is a human-made image. The symbol Johns makes is not decorative or abstract, nor does it evoke a worldspace, because it is oriented around its human-made meaning. The audience encountering the *Flag* paintings at the Leo Castelli Gallery in 1958 were shocked by the subject matter. The flags could have easily been accepted in the Dadaist and Surrealist tradition of assimilating previously existing designs and symbols into an art work, if Johns's flags were "assimilated." However, with the exception *of Flag Above White with Collage*, the viewer was provided with no alternative focus or overview. Placing the flag over a white field seemed to emphasize this difficulty. Another painting in Johns's first exhibition, *Three Flags*, which depicts nothing but the boundaries of larger American flags printed "behind" the American flag fully rendered, brought this problem of focus into the foreground.

Johns demonstrates that there is no center of interest or hierarchical focus possible when viewing a symbol. The symbol is merely construed as what it is. Cubist paintings allow their viewers to avoid this nature of symbols. The Cubists painted wine labels, tobacco packages, and other man-made signs as parts of a scene, however fragmented or barely suggested they were. Contrastingly, Johns gave his audience no escape but to recognize these signs as signs. Not only was he providing an antidote to the overt expressiveness of Abstract Expressionism, but, in offering the sign as subject matter, he graphically suggests that human-made illusions which represent reality are, if not the complete reality, as much of the objective world as we can understand. Our perceptions and conceptions can reach no further than our sign systems. Johns leads us to see our communications and languages in terms of form and media rather than any specific content. This concept becomes the keystone for much sixties thought and rhetoric, such as Marshall McLuhan's slogan, "the medium is the message." Without these ideas' proliferation into general intellectual consciousness, it is difficult for us to understand how alien Johns's flags, maps, and numbers seem a quarter of a century ago. Yet it is difficult to imagine the huge success of Pop Art if not for Johns.

After meeting Johns at a Frank O'Hara party in 1962 and then spending a great deal of time with the painter in his studio, Shapiro's poetry began to change.[20] The earliest poetry we have of his can be likened to an expressive Cubism. Shapiro would then tend most often to write about a subject from an emotional perspective, usually displaying contradictory feelings toward his subject, a poetic and inner analogue to the Cubist vision. These poems stuck to a particular scene, even if they may have changed almost every element in that scene. "Canticle" for example, can be viewed as a relatively conventional lyric when compared to Shapiro's later work, although the speaker's attitude toward his situation changes with little warning or reason:

> I was on a white coast once.
> My father was with me on his head.
>
> I said:
> Father, Father, I can't fall down,
> I was born for the sun and the moon.
>
> I looked at the clouds
> and all the clouds were mounting.
> My friends made a blue ring
> One hung down with the birds.
>
> (*J*1)

Compare "Canticle" to the more mature Shapiro's "The Page Turner," which begins with Clive Kilmister's epigraph, "Perhaps we can imagine a book like this one":

> The cover of the book is itself exactly
> Page one is you within a small room
> Page three already a fair field for your tomb
> Page four contains Newark matter-of-factly.
>
> Page five appropriates all its frightening streets
> On page six Greater Manhattan glumly fits
> There is room on page seven for all deceits
> And on page eight the earth comfortably sits.
> <div align="right">(<i>PT</i> 3)</div>

Here Shapiro matter-of-factly executes the double conceit of turning of the pages of a book to his life and the universe. Each one of his lines gets the job done like the kind of dispassionate encaustic brush stroke Johns uses to complete his *Flag*. "The cover of the book is itself exactly" is a tautology, yet serviceable for the poem.

Shapiro causes his readers to perceive the difference between the word and its meaning just as Johns stresses the distinction between sign and representational illusion when he, for instance, paints the stenciled letters "RE-D" over a yellow patch of color in his 1959 *False Start*. In the following stanza from "Venetian Blinds," there is no subject matter except language:

> One might call it tracing a hyacinth, or traces of a hyacinth.
> Like traces on a blackboard
> Or tracing the window from a neo-classicism upon a blackboard.
> These days that might as well not exist.
> <div align="right">(<i>TI</i> 37)</div>

Johns is careful to keep his painting within the realm of art. He predominantly uses recognizably artistic materials, like oil paint, encaustic, charcoal, and the printing process. When he collages objects into his work, the objects are either involved in the artistic process like the sculptural casts in *Target with Four Faces* or they are crafted, simple, human-made objects like a hanger, broom, or ruler. Also, Johns's painstakingly deliberate brushwork causes the viewer to consider his painting as painting in a conventional sense. However, for all the apparent effort in his brushwork, it attempts nothing. We might notice craft but it does not serve function, representation, emotion, or content. The painterliness of his brushstroke is at odds with the nonpainterliness of his subject matter.

Johns does not attempt to do more with painting than he feels painting is able to do. To him it would not only be false to lead his viewer into accepting a two-dimensional representation as three-dimensional but, reaching the root of the deception, avoids suggesting illusory space, or space which differs from the actual physical space, at all. Johns may employ painterly qualities, yet nonetheless sign, brushwork, and the actual physical plane that the painting occupies can all be easily differentiated from one another.

Shapiro apparently advocates this same kind of artistic honesty and he encounters the same self-limitations placed upon his expression. Yet, just as Johns's art can be said to concern perception, Shapiro's poetry can be understood as a meditation upon truth. Johns's perceptual truth lies in his artistic materials, actual sign (and on occasion actual "thing"), and his aversion to hiding his brushwork. Shapiro's linguistic truth lies in using language much the way it is found in everyday life. He does not merely refrain from imposing literal truth from "meaning anything"; he avoids it.

Johns annihilated illusory space, space which suggests the objective world, through the use of premade impersonal content and the sign-nature of his content. All language has something of this quality. Thus, whereas Johns constricted his subject matter, Shapiro expands his subject matter to the limits of his assimilative powers and beyond. After he met Johns, "language itself" asserted its supremacy over the poem's scene, situation, and/or emotion. For example, "A Family Slide" begins:

> Family on the slide, you should say!
> See if this slide fits—
> It rained yesterday; it rained today—
> I told you we had duplicates.
>
> (*PT* 38)

The poem opens with a rhetorical clarification but then moves into the narration *in medias res*. The third line, though painlessly beside the point, is not a pure non-sequitur because weather is perhaps the most commonplace of subjects and hence never wholly inappropriate. The fourth line is the poem's most surprising and begins to illustrate the manner in which language increasingly dominates Shapiro's poetry. The word "duplicates" diffuses the comment about the weather by emphasizing the recurring syntactical structure of "It rained yesterday; it rained today." While displaying the material of language, Shapiro merges metaphysical and tangible qualities. Are the "yesterday" and "today" of "A Family Slide's" third line entities? If days are like the words that represent them, they can be made, used, and duplicated.

The counter-pointing of "slide" and weather is not as recognizable as the ambiguity itself. However, the stanza is much more than ambiguous. It is a simple, easeful discourse in the form of an ABAB rhyming quatrain ("duplicates" comprises an off-rhyme with "fits"). Like Johns, who works within the craft and materials of conventional art, Shapiro at times uses simple, plain, unadorned speech and language but nonetheless uses poetic form paradoxically to freshen it further. For instance, "Master Canterel at Locus Solus" repeats the last line of each quatrain as the preceding one of the next. The effect is to designify and dedramatize as it parodies the poem's language. Poetic technique is used to make the poem less "framed":

> And nothing was missing
> Introduced into the brain
> The family is now watching
> The scene that's produced
>
> The scene that's produced
> Might be several different scenes
> Only the muscles are loosed
> With vitalium and resurrectine
>
> With vatalium and ressurectine
> They dress as they need to
> Outside the cooling machine
> Inside the grieving family
>
> Inside the grieving family
> Covered with heavy sweaters.
> (*PFD* 44)

Shapiro explores the assembling of disjunctive phrases in a manner resembling Johns's continual reworking of the same motifs. The difference is that "actual" visual subject matter is limited and language is not: our gaze takes in one fixed view, yet we can converse indefinitely. There is no logically imperative ending to Shapiro's long works. He overcomes this formlessness by either using modular or ongoing structural units, as with the quatrain in "The Devil's Trill Sonata," or by using "found" material selectively within a poetic framework.

John's work is art because it could be nothing else. It uses the traditional skills and materials peculiar to art and required to make art. However, it is almost as if Johns was "de-artifying" art and returning it to its medieval status as a craft and workmanlike activity, since the art leads to no expressive end, nor is it stimulated by any. One feels that Johns is making a painting to no ulterior purpose. Similarly, Shapiro employs as much poetic device as called for to ensure that a poem derived from a preexisting group of words will work as a poem. He is more the workman than expressive poet. An extreme example is "Screen" in which Shapiro focuses upon the listings under "screen" in *Roget's Thesaurus*:

> The window-shade
> is a small quantity
>
> Shades:
> —of death
> —of difference
> —of evening
>
> Shading
>   off
>
> into unsubstantial
>   copies
>
> small
> accompaniment
>
> It is thin,
> the window-shade
>
> and thin events
> come forth
>
> May your window-shade never
>   be less

> Your courtesy
>
> and your shadowy
>
> deep
>
> frame.
>
> (*L*)

Although there is little of Shapiro's personality in this poem there is an emotively moving quality in it. The dry material of *Roget's Thesaurus* works as a poem because of the line-breaking, spacing, and collaging with other material.

One coming to "Screen" without prior explanation would probably not guess it had its origin in a thesaurus, nor would a viewer recognize that Johns's *White Flag* is painted on newsprint, which is then placed upon canvas. However, in both works we must admit to an inescapable sense of "otherness." Although both artists may camouflage their tracks, they do not cover them. Shapiro may use his own spacing and interweave sections of the thesaurus in a distinctive fashion, just as Johns may paint an all-white American flag on pieces of newsprint dipped in wax and adhered upon canvas, yet the qualities of both the thesaurus and newsprint remain and, in a textural sense, dominate. Max Kozloff maintains that *White Flag* reverses the ordinary collage process in which the quality of the material is negated in favor of the quality of the illusion created.[21] Johns practically overlooks his artistic illusion, the American flag, in favor of the "semi-transparency" of newsprint blurred by paint and wax. Similarly, the words Shapiro "lifts" carry the reference book's seeming eternally real and objective character, and the poetic illusion he creates is inseparable from and dependent on it. This poetic illusion contains sentimentality, which is paradoxically in opposition to objectivity. In like manner, newsprint's faint recognizability suggests depth that opposes Johns's impasto paint handling protruding from the surface. This causes an uncanny tension in the painting which is really more significant than either quality, though a product of the play between them, just as tension created between objective and sentimental tones is more important than either in "Screen": "Shades: / —of death /—of difference /—of evening."

It should be mentioned that Johns has feigned an almost tongue-in-cheek indifference to aesthetic results. Asked why he put plaster cast faces atop his painted target in *Target with Four Faces*, Johns replied that they were just something he found in his studio. When asked why he cropped them just below the eyes, he said they needed to be that size to fit in the boxes.[22] It seems unlikely that his actions had so little rationale. Cage motivated Johns to adapt a watchful indifference to his work, yet Cage found that the rectangular shape of *Target with Four Faces* perfectly offset the circle of the target and that faces were just the right subject for what was left in the rectangle, being quite appropriate to focus upon, to offset the periphery's import and produce "a duplex asymmetrical structure."[23] Even Cage recognized an aesthetic intent in *Target with Four Faces*, though it hinged upon negation and paradox. Genuinely indifferent to the final aesthetic results, Cage might be intrigued by his products and appreciate them but he would never change a result after a process he has decided upon had rendered it, since he considers the process he employs to be of crucial import; therefore his introductions for his musical and artistic works might be regarded as part of their respective works. However, unlike Cage, Johns often has little to say about his work, which may speak for itself, yet what it speaks of is quite often the way it was made. As in Cage's work, process is of primary import, but Johns must manifest this process in a visually articulate form.

Shapiro's aesthetic standards include antithetical esteem for both found and poetically reworked language. Johns displays the same antithetical values by emphasizing how he remakes preexisting subject matter. This seemingly contrary manner of working which the two artists share may be at least partially motivated by their "realism"— not representationalism but the urge to make an honest example of what a work of art can be and do. Such "realism" compels them to find specimens of life as it seemingly is. Although anything might in some sense fulfill this task, two related problems emerge. First, objects or words change because they are considered art. They are taken out of context, and our preconceptions of what art is alters our perception of it. Second, the object or words will be unnaturally isolated. The environmental or contextual change will produce something not only less "real" than the original thing but also something that is perhaps less real than illusionist art, whether it be abstract or representational. In accordance with their senses of honesty, Johns and Shapiro must devise stratagems to enliven their work as exemplified by life and "things as they are" when viewed as an artwork or read as a poem.

It is impossible to write representation-free poetry. Yet Shapiro confounds sense and astonishes because he attains consistently arresting and dynamic results while writing poetry that discursively and dynamically goes nowhere. Jasper Johns and David Shapiro, both representing the second wave of a generation of New York School artists, acknowledge the impossibility of poetry and painting accurately to recreate truth and objective reality; both favor the use of the found or given or preexisting in their respective arts as a way of basing their works on certain truth and making nonillusionist art that is not merely abstract; the painter and poet share the influence of John Cage, produce personal yet unintentional art, and recreate or doctor their respective found materials according to means recognizable as art.

The 1980s marked a shift in Johns's and Shapiro's work. Johns's *In the Studio* (1982) suggests the possibility of painting which is suggestive of space, perspective, and imitation of a worldspace. The painting presents a drawing table with the distance between lines representing the width of the drawing table attenuated towards the top so as to create perspective. Perspective implies that someone is watching. Thus as an antithesis of this perspective creating a new synthesis, Johns places a long piece of wood approximately one-inch wide on the canvas. This wood droops from a hook. A latch has been inserted into the back of the wood. Since the wood is attached to the canvas from the upper portion of the wood, gravity pulls the lower part toward the canvas and the upper part falls away from the canvas the approximate two inches which is the length of the hook. This tilted but vertical wood suggests a ruler though there are no measurements inscribed upon it, suggesting a lack of substance in contemporary political rulers.

Johns seems to be comfortable with suggesting perspective only because the seeming ruler seems to be the factor to which the perspective stands in relation. The painting, therefore, seems true to itself because the observer is suggested within the painting.

As Johns has been trying to cope with the possibilities of perspective without renouncing the thrust of his prior work, so Shapiro has been attempting to make statements within his poetry. For instance, in the title poem of *To An Idea*, there is a long, "familiar" dedication:

> To an idea, writ in water,
> To wild flesh, on the surface alone.
> To you who carried me like mail
> From one house to another,
> Now the cars go past the lake, as if copying could exist.
> The signs shine, through the Venetian blinds.
>
> (*TI* 15)

Earlier in the poem, Shapiro states a doctrine of his objectives, "to know nothing,/to taste something, dazzled by absence." These objectives approximate the aims he has long held to, that the fullness of the truth can be better experienced and a poem be more truthful without a poet's intentions being directly expressed. However, since it is contradictory to say one should know nothing, Shapiro does not state "I know nothing," but rather, "to know nothing" and, before he does, he uses a third of the poem to qualify his doctrine before it is announced. His doctrine is further set, in a confusing fashion, by ending the poem with a long dedication. Thus, by pronouncing the fact that his sentiments are written and contained in a poem, Shapiro is writing his own opinions as he seems to find them, just as Johns creates perspective that seems to be a natural function of an element within his work. The world writes itself through a David Shapiro poetry. If the poem had an ego, it would lose it in its inherently semiotic qualities. Shapiro's poetry is informed by the discrete (and in some ways the discreet) nature of reading signs and hence bridges New York School and Language poetry.

NOTES

1. Frank O'Hara, *The Collected Poems of Frank O'Hara*, ed. Donald Allen (New York: Knopf, 1971), 512.

2. Edwin Denby, *Homage to Frank O'Hara*, eds., Bill Berkson and Joe LeSuer (Berkeley: Creative Arts Books, 1980), 32.

3. Leo Steinberg, *Other Criteria* (New York: Oxford University Press, 1972), 83–84.

4. Ibid., 85.

5. Although David Shapiro befriended many of the same artists of the first generation as the New York School poets did, as well as younger artists, when he moved to New York City in 1964, he also published in many literary magazines. "First generation" poets facilitated Shapiro's notoriety in the poetry world when, at fourteen, in 1961, he began writing the poems that were to be compiled in his

first book, *January* (1965). As I learned through an unpublished interview with him (Oct. 30, 1981), historical influences were filtered to Shapiro through his older friends. For major historical predecessors Shapiro, like Kenneth Koch, has cited the work of Baudelaire and the French Symbolists; like Frank O'Hara; the great Russian poets of before and after their revolution; and, like John Ashbery, Wallace Stevens.

If Ashbery, O'Hara, and Koch affected Shapiro more than any other living poets, perhaps Larry Rivers and the Abstract Expressionists provided indirect models for Shapiro as well. However, a sharply defined new factor arose in the art world in between the early 1950s, which were the formative years for Shapiro's predecessors, and the early 1960s when Shapiro found his style. Johns and Rauschenberg undoubtedly were the focal point for a dramatic shift of sensibility inside the New York and international artistic communities during the late 1950s and early 1960s.

6. Calvin Tomkins, *Robert Rauschenberg and the Art World of Our Time* (New York: Penguin, 1980), 116.

7. Ibid., 117.

8. Harold Bloom, *Saturday Review* (December 1977), 83.

9. Unpublished interview with David Shapiro, October 30, 1981.

10. Frank O'Hara, *Lunch Poems* (San Francisco: City Lights, 1964), 35–36.

11. Leo Steinberg, *Other Criteria*, 86–87.

12. Calvin Tomkins, *The Bride and the Bachelors* (New York: Penguin Books, 1962), 91.

13. Ibid.

14. Ibid.

15. Ibid., 99.

16. Ibid., 100.

17. Ibid., 101.

18. Leo Steinberg, *Other Criteria*, 90.

19. Ibid., 91.

20. Unpublished interview with David Shapiro, October 30, 1981.

21. Max Kozloff, *Jasper Johns* (New York: Abrams, 1967),16.

22. Leo Steinberg, *Other Criteria*, 31–32, 35–36.

23. John Cage, "Jasper Johns: Stories and Ideas," *The New Art*, ed. Gregory Battcock (New York: E.P. Dutton & Co., 1966), 219.

Shapiro's Comedic Poetics and Its Limits in *Harrisburg Mon Amour, or Two Boys on a Bus*

Daniel Morris

Harrisburg Mon Amour, or Two Boys on a Bus is a lyrical drama—described in the play as an "interior dialogue"—cowritten in 1979–80 by David Shapiro (b. 1947) and his former student at Columbia, the poet and critic Stephen Paul Miller (b. 1951). It is somewhat misleading to describe the play as "written" by the "two boys," Shapiro and Miller, because the script is in fact an often garbled and yet verbatim transcription of a cassette recording—the transcript is over one hundred pages long—of a conversation that took place in April 1979 aboard a Thruways Bus from the Port Authority in New York City to Kutztown, Pennsylvania, where both men were scheduled to give poetry readings at Kutztown University.

A collaborative play, and not a poem, *Harrisburg* remains a valuable text to discuss in this volume because of the light it sheds on Shapiro's poetics and especially his relationship to the metamorphic poetics of other New York School authors of a prior generation such as Kenneth Koch and John Ashbery. Like Shapiro in the play under discussion, Koch and Ashbery participated in collaborative works of art, theater, and music with such artists as Larry Rivers and Alex Katz. A treatment of Shapiro's poetics would thus be incomplete without a commentary on his experimentation with collaborative authorship via the multimediated, dramatic, and yet playful performance of the spoken word that is a signature feature of avant-garde practices and the New York School aesthetics in which he participates in the play. In *Harrisburg*, Shapiro's performance text challenges traditional conceptions of realist drama, blurring the line between poetry and performance, art and life. In the process, he causes us to rethink traditional ideas about dramatic characterization through the deconstruction of the major personae in the play.

In *Harrisburg*, Shapiro illustrates his allegiance to a fundamental tenet of Ashberian poetics—the desire to defer the long association in Western metaphysics between writing, and especially poetry writing, and the absent, violated, or disembodied self. Instead of accepting the tragic replacement of linguistic image for the vanished self—the "terrible beauty" described by Yeats at the conclusion of "Easter 1916"—Shapiro's collaborative effort with Miller attempts to reconcile art with immanence through verbatim transcription of the often incoherent and yet at times profoundly thought-provoking manic chatter that is *Harrisburg*. As the poet and theorist Allen Grossman has said of the "confessional" poetry of Robert Lowell, Miller and Shapiro situate their play "at the point of intersection between the life lived and the transcendental exactions of art."[1]

As Grossman has also argued about Lowellian poetics, and as the parodic and metafictional elements of *Harrisburg* reveal, such a project may not satisfy some readers because it offers "no meaning and no end . . . confers no consolation" and "yields no story but the account of its own production."[2] At the same time, there are rich rewards to attempts by Ashbery, Lowell, and Shapiro and Miller in *Harrisburg* to imagine a nontragic or comic poetics. For *Harrisburg* offers a refreshing alternative to the death-dealing poetics evident within foundational Western texts such as the *Gilgamesh*, the *Gospels*, or the *Iliad*, where Achilles hesitates inside a tent before agreeing to rescue the disfigured body of Patroklus because Achilles understands full well the deadly trade off of more life for lines in a memorable poem that will occur once he steps foot on the battlefield against the Trojans.

As Grossman says of Ashbery, and as is true for authors such as Shapiro working in the comedic tradition, contemporary poets are able "to search the resources of discourse without ever allowing them to complete themselves. [Authors such as Ashbery and Shapiro] disencumber themselves of the terrors of history, not by reinventing the world in a new way but by allowing no argument of the past to complete its tragic implications."[3] The manic quality of the improvisation between Shapiro and Miller in *Harrisburg* speaks to their fear of closure, of completion, of silence as a sign of ending, as well as of their desire to defer textual cessation in order to avoid the association between literary form and representational violence—that is to say, the tragic exchange of natural being for art. The play thus privileges talking, associated with natural presence, at least in pre-Derridean thought, over writing, (associated with an evacuation of natural presence in favor of the permanence of art).

As noted, the *Harrisburg* transcript is itself imperfect. It is a stammering, often incoherent trace of what transpired between Miller and Shapiro during the long bus ride between the Port Authority and Kutztown. The incompleteness of the transcript suggests the inability of art to finally contain the presence of the "two boys," whose yammering spills out of the text, remaining unruly, uncontrollable, and unrepresentable. At times, the transcriber notes, loud traffic sounds or other noises infiltrate the recording, disallowing an accurate rendering of what is being said by the main interlocutors. At other times—hundreds of other times over the course of the script—the transcriber resorts to question marks instead of words because the cassette's sound is so unclear that reception of thought is blocked, deferring the closure that understanding signifies:[4]

> Miller: I don't know. She had told me that my poetry was beautiful, and she said ???? And she stressed that sexuality—
> Shapiro: Mastery, sometimes, is what people mean by "Beauty." Beauty is ???? to be power."

The aporias, blanks, interruptions, and unfinished thoughts become strangely meaningful and thematically significant, even as they frustrate the reader/listener who becomes interested in following the discussion's twists and turns before key moments of thought and expression are erased by the outside noises.

Ashbery attempts to challenge the stability of the lyric "I," or the singularity of the authorial perspective. In "Litany" from *As We Know* (1979), Ashbery instructs in an "Author's Note" that, the poem's "two columns . . . are meant to be read as simultaneous but independent monologues."[5] Similarly, in *Harrisburg Mon Amour*, Miller and Shapiro attempt to remove the authorial "I" from agency as the shaping force of the drama. They do so by following avant-garde filmmakers from the 1960s such as Goddard and Warhol in offering a chattering version of "cinema verité" in which a cassette recording of what Shapiro in the play calls "2 people thinking about poetry . . . thinking about art and poetry" (*HMA* Act 2, 19) in an unfiltered, unscripted manner replaces the conscious shaping of the work by the singular authorial imagination. As in the music of John Cage, himself a major influence on Ashbery and other members of the New York School in the 1950s, chance operations replace the ego as the shaping force in the play.

Stylistically, then, *Harrisburg* mocks traditional ideas of lyric closure, of the idea of the finished work of art, as well as privileging the written over the spoken word:

> Shapiro: I would much rather have T.S. Eliot, rather than writing *The Cocktail Party*, talking about art and poetry. Those would have been a terrific play that he didn't write. Or if Wallace Stevens, rather than "A Cat On Broomstick," had really written just about poetry.
> (*HMA* Act 2, 18–19)

As with Ashbery, upon whom Shapiro has written an important critical study, Shapiro and Miller avoid a self-expressionist ethos in *Harrisburg* by deferring closure and by offering multiple masks of themselves in the play.

> Shapiro: Someone said to Ashbery, "Where is there room for self-expression in your work?" He pointed to the signature at the bottom and said, "That's the place for self-expression." But still . . . you know De Kooning said he paints himself out of the painting, then he knows it's finished.
> (*HMA* Act 2, 27)

Shortly after Shapiro's recollection of Ashbery's depersonalization of the lyric, Miller and Shapiro break out of their autobiographical personae in an outrageous way. For a portion of the play, they reimagine themselves as a variety of cultural and historical figures ranging from Mozart to Rimbaud, to Caesar to Santayana. A humorous portion of Act 2, for example, is devoted to mock interviews between Mozart (Shapiro) and Caesar (Miller). Here is Shapiro as Mozart:

> I haven't taken any boats, you know I keep going by carriage—Vienna, Paris. . . . Sometimes I feel—I've said this some place else, but sometimes I feel as if I've seen the interior of every castle on the map. I was dragged from age four over the mountains of Europe.
> (*HMA* Act 2, 35–36)

Shapiro's Mozart is absurdly funny and poignant at the same time. Himself a prodigy violinist who decided against a career as a professional musician in favor of the life of the poet-scholar-teacher evident in the verbal performance in the play, Shapiro offers a strangely moving assessment of what the young Mozart's life must really have been like, being pulled like a freakish circus performer from place to place by primitive forms of transportation.

Shapiro and Miller upset traditional dramatic structures by upsetting notions of authorial intent and by blurring the outlines of their dramatic personae. They also parody the idea of managing narrative time in a rigid formula, thus suggesting that experience cannot be neatly divided into the beginning, middle, and end typical of most dramatic fictions in an Aristotelian or Chekhovian mode. "Act 1" ends, rather abruptly, on the forty-third page, in the midst of a lengthy discussion about the nature of the beautiful and its relationship to the ridiculous and the destructive. (All three are important and interrelated themes throughout the play.) One presumes "act 1" ceases simply because the cassette tape has run its course, and so it seemed to Miller and Shapiro a reasonable place to offer a ten-minute intermission.

The rest of the play consists of another sixty-eight pages of dialogue, but it is misleading to describe what follows as "act 2" because the authors/dialogists within the script consciously disrupt linear time frames in favor of an improvisational technique that emphasizes the unpremeditated "flow" of thought and language. Dreams, jokes, puns, themes, and observations about philosophical issues such as the nature of love, beauty, and art develop and recur between the "two boys on a bus" as they travel in the cramped, often claustrophobic quarters of an interstate bus as it rambles through industrial New Jersey and into the pastoral fields of Pennsylvania. Act 2 begins with Shapiro stating:

> This is Act II of Harrisburg Mon Amour. We could have put it Act 47. . . . And as a matter of fact, did the last act have a beginning, middle and end . . . or did it have it in a reverse order as Goddard said? Did it just have an emergency exit; do we let it just fall—Do we let it fall properly the way that you said? We could spend this whole act analyzing the other act; that's what Hamlet does.
>
> (*HMA*, Act 2, 1)

The fact that Taylor Mead, best known as a performer in Andy Warhol's real time films from the "Factory" in the late 1960s, played the Miller persona *and* the Shapiro persona in his well-received performances of Harrisburg at The Kitchen in New York City in 1980, further illustrates the metamorphic fluidity of identity, the way in which self and other collide and combine into something else or someone else in the course of the play's literal and figurative journeys.[6] As the idea of a long bus journey suggests, the Odyssean poetics of this play favors the rich ongoingness of unscripted play and the unexpected illuminations that occur when conversation between literate and thoughtful friends takes place in an unfiltered manner.

Parodic role-playing might seem a mere distraction from the drudgery of the long distance bus trip with little significance to an analysis of Shapiro's poetics were it not for the fact that it is in the course of play-acting one of the main dramatic events—the spilling of a grape drink onto Shapiro's pants—occurs:

> Shapiro: I probably completely stained my pants with grape juice. It's been a disaster. Turn on the thing [the tape recorder]; It's very Chekhovian. . . . Doesn't grape juice stain forever?
> Miller: It's wet, but I don't think it's stained. It's mostly water, and anyway, your jacket covers it.
> Shapiro: And I brought other pants, but I think it's been an amazing sacrifice for art . . . . I'm no longer Mozart. Now I'm in grape-stained pants.
>
> (*HMA*, Act 2, 36–37)

The screwball comedy is here deadpan and really very funny as we observe the scenario of the two guys panicking about what they are going to wear to the upcoming reading at Kutztown, and what they are going to eat, drink, and read for the rest of the long trip now that the tuna sandwiches and The *Village Voice* have been drenched in grape drink. The questions of "will it stain" and what will Shapiro wear at the reading become the source of pages of obsessive commentary. As silly and parodic as is the situation, Shapiro is making a point about the limits to his comedic project, which is the desire to produce a kind of artless text that does not require loss or pain to produce imaginative language or narrative momentum. Towards the end of the play, then, when an episode on the bus creates a rare moment of "action," or the sense of something happening (other than talking), it is described as a tragic (Chekhovian) moment.

The desire to get the ego out of the way of art is certainly at play in the shifting from Miller-Shapiro to Caesar-Mozart. The reality of the vulnerable physical bodies and the cramped quarters in which the two characters reside as the bus travels from New York City to Kutztown, however, intrudes upon the authorial fantasy that the self can be infinitely transferable, infinitely translatable, to other times and other places and to other selves. The main dramatic event in the play entails an injury—a blood-like stain that produces social as well as economic distress—as Shapiro struggles to figure out what he is going to wear to the real life performance of his poems in Kutztown, and whether he has the money to buy new clothes when he gets there: "So there was a disaster. Life was a disaster. I probably completely stained this entire suit—seventy-dollar suit. . . . Oh no, it might be two hundred, you know" (*HMA*, Act 2, 39).

The free play of language and of identities attempts to get the violence out of representation, but the reality of life, of gravity, of the fact that things fall off of bus racks and make a mess, and destroy expensive suits just before you are supposed to appear in public, wake us up from such illusions. Throughout the play, manic chatter signifies the desire to stave off the disaster of art through a poetics of endless play, endless parody, endless non-seriousness. In the end, however, the bus will stop, the "boys" will need to return to their real life situation as the "men" that Kutztown has invited to the stage.

The title of the play alludes to the Alain Resnais film *Hiroshima mon amour* (1959), in which a French young woman has spent the night with a Japanese man, at Hiroshima where she went for the shooting of a film about peace. He reminds her of the first man she loved. It was during World War II, and he was a German soldier. The main themes of this film are memory and oblivion. The transcript of Shapiro's play, however, reads like a cross between *My Dinner with André* (1981) and the movie *Speed* (1994), starring Keanu Reeves as Officer Jack Traven, a young cop who must save the passengers of a bus that has a bomb set to explode if the bus goes below fifty miles per hour. Reeves thus needs to keep the bus in motion, without breaking, as he winds the bus through cluttered city streets to avoid a disaster.

Structurally and thematically, *Harrisburg* anticipates *Speed*. The end point of the play is the arrival at Kutztown, associated in the minds of the playwright/characters with the nuclear meltdown of Three Mile Island and the fear of the "China Syndrome" depicted in the 1978 Jane Fonda/Jack Lemmon/Michael Douglas film of that name. The end of the bus trip, then, the end of the cassette recording, signifies in the play the end of the real time presence of Miller and Shapiro and their transformation into characters, into artifacts in the completed transcript. (As Shapiro states in a moving reminiscence of the death of his mother, his desire to tape record her words will not put a stay to physical deterioration).

Like Louis Malle's *My Dinner with André*, one could argue that virtually nothing happens in *Harrisburg Mon Amour*, with the exception of two friendly acquaintances sitting together to talk for an extended period of time—the time it takes to eat a slowly paced meal in a fine restaurant in New York City in the case of *My Dinner with André*, the longer time it takes to travel on the interstate bus from the Port Authority to Kutztown in the play. In both film and play, one of the participants—André Gregory in *My Dinner*, Shapiro in *Harrisburg*—does more of the talking—and the other participant—Wallace Shawn, Stephen Paul Miller—contributes to the conversation through some talking, some questioning, but also as a sympathetic and collegial listener to the other in the dialogic space. In both *André* and *Harrisburg* the dialogue produces an internal transformation in the characters. In some ways, then, both document the archetypal (Socratic) scene of the teacher and student learning together through conversation about crucial issues, such as the nature of beauty, the nature of love, and the relationship of art to experience.

In *My Dinner with André*, André Gregory, the New York theater director, has just survived a harrowing experience in which he was buried alive as part of a ceremony. Returning to the city, he wishes to share this experience with Shawn, whose mundane existence is such that he expresses happiness at finding that a fly has not fallen into his cold cup of coffee when he wakes up to it after a night of rest. In *Harrisburg*, Shapiro may not transmit to Miller so strange an experience as a mock burial, but in fact Shapiro, then at Columbia University, had been Miller's teacher, both are traveling outside the safety of their home spaces, and one senses that Shapiro, the teacher, is taking his protégé to Kutztown to share a stage, but also to offer the talented student the opportunity to collaborate in a form of performance art on the way to the stage.

The fact that Miller's major long speech in the play, which Shapiro describes as "a kind of ecstatic moment in which you rise like Socrates beyond" (*HMA*, Act 2, 67) takes place right before the bus reaches Kutztown, suggests the long conversation has been transformed into an empowering moment for Miller. Throughout much of the play, Shapiro does tend to dominate the conversation, often cutting in to Miller's thoughts before he has the chance to develop them for himself. But then at the end Shapiro steps back to allow Miller to shine in a monologue about the Indian guru Meher Baba's slippery teachings on "truth" ("The truth is what helps people") and about how Baba taught his own sister a paradoxical lesson about managing life's many tasks by suggesting she learn how to "hurry up" and "slow down" at the same time (*HMA*, Act 2, 66–68). Miller's concluding monologue thus illustrates the noble teacher-student model that Shapiro has fostered, one of sharing and then empowerment.

The play ends on a positive note in terms of the teacher-student relationship through Miller's speech, but overall *Harrisburg* emphasizes the power of death and destruction to dismantle the authors' hope to preserve life through art. In fact, art is understood throughout the play as itself a destructive element in human life. As noted, Shapiro and Miller struggle with the question of how to get the violence out of representation by putting an end to the age old association between representational significance and death. The point is made quite directly in the play through a discussion of Christ's sacrifice, but also in a very literal sense related to the cassette recording of the discussion that becomes the transcript for the play.

It seems the cassette tape upon which Miller has chosen to record the conversations is, inadvertently, the same tape that contains, not only contemporary music, but also a rare recording of a fellow poet's work. The technical means to record one event thus directly impinges upon the recollection of a prior event, which is, quite literally, erased to make room for the appearance of the new conversation.

> Miller: You know I hope we're not tape-recording—
> (silence)
> Shapiro: We're back to your play. We just realized that the play has destroyed that.
> Miller: The Henri Murcher tape has been gone, everything for the one moment that was on. (*HMA*, Act 1, 26)

Miller and Shapiro understand representation of the spoken word as a scarce resource, a zero-sum game in which memory is directed to one scene (usually associated with violence and death) at the expense of recalling another. Shapiro connects the play's obsession with defining the beautiful to the theme of mutilation:

> In what sense was it a moment? So we've mutilated the beautiful. Maybe one way you can find out about the beautiful, is if you get a sensation that you've destroyed it, and Heidegger says you only know being as being forgets itself and being towards death. Maybe this is a Heideggerian moment for you, Stephen Paul Miller.
> (*HMA*, Act 1, 26–27).

Harrisburg Mon Amour, or Two Boys on a Bus is untidy, riotously so, and "blemished," to use a phrase from the text that is associated with love, beauty, and attraction. The imperfect script, recorded as it is over the prior recording of another poet's voice, now erased and lost, however, suggests an important aspects of Shapiro's comedic poetics—art's inability to fully recover or accurately contain the momentum of living speech without producing unrecoverable loss and pain.

Notes

1. Allen Grossman, *The Sighted Singer: Two Works on Poetry for Readers and Writers.* (Baltimore: Johns Hopkins University Press, 1992), 30.
2. Ibid.
3. Ibid., 44.
4. David Shapiro and Stephen Paul Miller, *Harrisburg Mon Amour, or Two Boys on a Bus*, unpublished typescript, 1979–1980, Act 2, 4. Further quotations from *Mon Amour, or Two Boys on a Bus* are cited in the text as *HMA*; when lines are sufficiently located, no citation appears.
5. John Ashbery, *As We Know* (New York: Penguin, 1979), 2.
6. The play included sound by Laurie Anderson and sets by Linda Francis.

Plays Well with Others: The Collaborative Poetry of David Shapiro

Denise Duhamel

DAVID SHAPIRO OFTEN WRITES POEMS THAT ARE PLURALISTIC, POLYphonic, with shifting pronouns and quick leaps that change points of view. Because of this and his affiliation with the New York School, he is an ideal candidate for collaborative experiments. He peppers these cowritten poems, many of which are written with children, freely within his "own" books.

Most notable are Shapiro's poems written with his son Daniel. There's an author's photo of Shapiro in which he carries Daniel on his shoulders, gripping Daniel's ankles, grounding him, as Daniel looks up and points to the sky. David himself looks straight into the camera, smiling for both of them. The father/son photo seems to illustrate their poetic process, as many of these Shapiro/Shapiro poems underline an obsession with God who they presume is up there, beyond the clouds toward which Daniel is looking. The poems ask: *Who is God, and what is he up to?* In an interview with Elizabeth Bassford, Shapiro relates this story: "I recently heard a girl went up to Borges and said, 'Señor Borges, do you believe in God?' And he took both her hands and said, 'I am such a skeptic, I cannot rule out the possibilities'."[1] And neither can David Shapiro.

The Shapiro/Shapiro poems in which God becomes a character ("The Car in a Maze," "The World in God," "God's Shadow," "Black Silk," in *A Burning Interior* and sections 7. 'God Meets the Angel' and 8. 'The Boss Poem' from a longer, predominantly noncollaborative poem called "Voice" in *After a Lost Original*) are written in simple syntax with short, mostly declarative lines. The poems are simultaneously unpretentious, and surprisingly multilayered and mysterious.

While it is impossible to know what lines in these poems were written by the child and what lines were written by the father, the symbiotic questions and assertions addressed in these poems underscore the wisdom of children and playfulness of which adults, especially adult poets, are capable. "God Meets the Angel" begins:

> Flying with my flying wings
> Flying in my flying wings
> I'm flying and I'm going to see God
> I'm going to see God now.
> (*ALO* 61)

The speaker here becomes Daniel daydreaming atop of David's shoulders, David (or someone with an adult sensibility) pondering death, a third speaker rejoicing in the rapture, an angel of the title perhaps. Or the speaker is a chorus singing a revisionist spiritual. A reader can easily imagine these four lines sung by a choir in the style of *Swing Low, Sweet Chariot*. Indeed, Thomas Fink has written: "Rather than being 'anti-grammar,' Shapiro often pushes for 'Utopian alternative grammar' that abandons unitary utterance for multiplicity."[2] The speaker in "God Meets the Angel" is omnipresent, just as God is presumed to be omnipresent. He/she/they are both flying "with" and "in" the wings. In the same poem, God is grand ("everywhere") and also miniscule:

> Angels are so little
> God is little
> like milkweed
> like little seeds.
> (*ALO* 61)

There is a deep spirituality and longing in these lines in addition to a fantastic Gulliver's Travel-esque quality. The child and adult sensibility fuse, as do the religious and secular.

"The Boss Poem" also deals with the ubiquitous nature of what we call "God." The poem-section in its entirety reads:

> Are you the boss of God?
> You are the boss of God?
> Nobody is the boss of God
> Not me not you

> Are the angels the boss of God?
> Are you more famous than angels?
> God orders himself
> To do what he wants
> I am the boss of this poem
> I wrote it.
>
> (*ALO* 62)

One reason children (and adults) are drawn to *Gulliver's Travels* and *Alice in Wonderland* is because of the power shifts that occur when the physical size of the characters are manifested. "The Boss Poem" could be read as a poem about ego (the writer's ego, especially) or about a child (or a childlike adult) asserting his/her presence and creativity. The poem's tone is one of a tough bravado: "Nobody is the boss of God / Not me not you. . . ." The idea that writers create their own universe in a poem is explored, freshly and with humor, in the final two lines. The questions throughout are used as a taunt, with an implied answer of "yes" after the first line. When the speaker asks, "Are you more famous than angels?" the speaker and the reader are humbled—and here the answer had better be "no." While there is a back and forth conversational quality, this poem—it is easy to imagine it dramatized with two speakers—can also be read as one poet's quarrel with the self.

Another Shapiro/Shapiro poem that uses the interrogative effectively is "The World in God." This time, in a seemingly self-mocking tone, Shapiro/Shapiro write:

"Why do people say God all time? / Why do I write poems about God always?" (*BI* 44).

But rather than becoming exhausted and annoyed with their questions, Shapiro and Shapiro answer themselves with all sincerity:

> because God is a good word to say
> because God is like silk on the moon
>
> God is like a flower in space
> and an angel is like a rose.
>
> (*BI* 44)

Here, the child's voice emerges purely. The wonder and strange logic is seen especially in the first two lines of "The World in God": "The whole world is in God's head / That is why he is so smart that's why he is so big" (*BI* 44). The second line's run-on sentence perfectly matches the breathiness of a child or a childlike proclamation, an "aha" moment that contrasts beautifully with the smallness of God when he is portrayed in "God Meets the Angel" as "like milkweed / like little seeds" (*ALO* 61).

Other similes that Shapiro / Shapiro use for God include: "God is like two angels," ("God's Shadow," *BI* 46); "God is like a black leaf," "God is like a window with two colors," and "God is like the veins / in the black leaves" ("Black Silk," *BI* 47). These constant comparisons, these constant attempts to define, are reminiscent of how a child learns: the new concept based on something already known. What saves these poems, of course, from the didacticism found in many poems in which God is called upon is that a definitive answer never evolves. Joanna Fuhrman has written, "To read a David Shapiro poem is to enter a space in which 'emotion' is as abstract as theory and an 'idea' is as visceral and tender as the best pop song."[3] God is indeed made visceral, if elusive, in these collaborations.

The power and awe Shapiro and Shapiro assign to God can also be read, to a certain extent, as astonishment assigned to nature. In "Black Silk" it is God who "makes the black leaf / fall from the rain" (*BI* 47). But the fluttering leaf in itself is cause for praise and celebration, as God is similar to the beauty of the leaves' veins. In "The Car in a Maze," Shapiro and Shapiro write, "God stays where he is" and, later, "Angels like to get lost in God—God is never lost" (48). This persistence of God in all things and this faith that there is some kind of plan are undercut only with the slightest of irony, in the ending line, "I like to get lost in my house." In this poem, unlike in "The Boss Poem," there is a sense that Shapiro and Shapiro are glad they are not God and rejoice in being lost (lambs), lost in their faith, less than perfect.

The irony continues and complicates itself in the 2002 "God's Shadow," one of the most recent Shapiro / Shapiro poems discussed here. Here, the second stanza of the poem turns decidedly political:

> God's shadow looks like two angels
> Flying out
> Flying to Somalia
> Kids are dying
> Their bones are white as teeth
> Their bones are red as the sun

> They are thin and God says
> Drink this milk and you will get stronger
> Strong as crystal
> And I will give you homes in Somalia
> That shine with darkness and pearls.
>
> *(BI* 46)

Father and son have seemed to grow up, but still have the capacity for whimsy and hope. Shapiro and Shapiro point out God's failure, not with anger, but with restraint. The speaker fantasizes that God will save the children of Somalia, even though His "shadow looks like two angels," which suspiciously, at least to this reader, look like two warplanes. The innocent speaker in "God Meets the Angel" who is "flying in my flying wings . . . going to see God" (*ALO* 61) has a head on collision with an ineffectual God who may or may not be "flying out to Somalia." The speaker is disappointed with God who "has a happy life," and yet is still humbled by God and God's impenetrability.

David Shapiro is aware of the unusual and thorny use of God in his poems, yet feels it is important work. He says in the Bassford interview, "Once John Ashbery wrote to me and he said he was amazed I had used the word God. It felt to him, 'as if a great human need were being addressed.'"

In two earlier Shapiro collaborations from *A Man Holding an Acoustic Panel*—one written with Renée and another with Paula, two children he worked with in the "Poets in the Schools" system—the tone and diction are even more childlike than those written with Daniel. In "Poem," collaborator Paula also becomes the main character, a girl who:

> . . . just kept jumping on the rope
> and she kept slipping
> and they threw her up in the night.
>
> (*MHAP* 39)

Here, "up" where Daniel was pointing in the photograph, Paula meets Jesus, not a kind and gentle Jesus, but a Jesus who "ate her up." This devouring Jesus apparently vomits the girl back up whole: "and she was so sad because she couldn't come back down / and she was happy because she came back down" (*MHAP* 39). The mystery of what happens between these two lines is never explained. And, again, the breathless simplistic syntax carries the strange and disturbing narrative as a small child might deliver it. Carl Whithaus has noted that "within the space of Shapiro's poems, we meet uncanny images and our attention is called to the surface of words, while the 'depth' of narrative or confession is exposed as illusion. Yet, and perhaps paradoxically, memory, the past, and history are always already present in the surface of Shapiro's poems."[4] The poems' surfaces are complicated (rippled, if you will) by the presence of a collaborator. The horror of childhood experience, the feeling of having no control over one's body and one's location, is further explored with the final stanza that refers to some kind of hell, possibly the hell of domesticity:

> and she was down down down in the fire
> and they cooked her in a hot house
> and she was burning and the hot house blew up the fire
> and she was married.
>
> (*MHAP* 39)

The echo of the hothouse flower heard in "hot house," the delicacy and balance of the hothouse, is instead an inferno that blows up. This is a torturous place, and Paula becomes the burning child, the unrescued Gretel left in the witch's oven. The "smiling Paula" of the first stanza is gone. The child of this poem is abandoned, abducted, and unable to control her own fate. The horror of the narrative is at odds with its singsong rhythms. God is not a particularly benevolent presence in this poem. Rather, He appears (through Jesus) as a punitive patriarchal figure. There is also interesting gender play here—Jesus eats Paula; Paula does not eat the body of Christ.

Similar gender reversals occur in "About a Farmer Who was Just a Little Boy" (with Renée), a romp of a poem that mimics a child's free associations. The characters of the poem (a farmer, a bride, a mommy, and a little boy named Tommy) all seem to shape-shift, blend and become one another. For example, the sixth stanza begins: "Then after that after a couple of years / He was sad because he wasn't a bride anymore" (*MHAP* 38). Later, the characters appear to switch roles: "Then the bride Stevie was a farmer." Identities blur and overlap: the child becomes the dead farmer come back to life, the bride becomes the mommy of the farmer instead of the wife. As in the Shapiro / Shapiro poems, "About a Farmer who was just a Little

Boy" also concerns itself with characters changing size: "And he ate as much dinner as he could / He blew up to be BIG BIG BIG / He was as big as my daddy" and later in the poem, "And the bride blew up / To be as big as my daddy" (*MHAP* 37).

This *Alice in Wonderland* theme is picked up again in "IV," a poem written in 2003 by David Shapiro and punk pioneer Richard Hell. Though this poem is written by two adults, size as metaphor is used throughout. The poem begins:[5]

> Let's make something smaller,
> small as a ring or an old riddle,
> smaller than things with charm,
> small and even smaller than her arm,
> smaller than a body part,
> and always a part of something smaller,
> as she said, I am always part
> of something smaller—"Don't hate
> me because I'm a small, small thing"

The "she" in the poem is assured: "she'd still rule my heart whatever her physical stature." The poem celebrates the diminutive, the child, and the delight in what is found in smallness. The child (or small woman) becomes the essence, the core, someone valuable and precise, which in turn becomes a metaphor for the essence of an idea as the poem ends:[6]

> Whatever's required: thoughts
> extend, they multiply, tangling
> frantically, to get the further small.

David Shapiro's willingness to collaborate with children and adults, to subsume his voice in service of the poem, is one of his main strengths as a writer. His collaborative work informs his solo work and vice versa. Jane Miller, in talking about her collaborations with Olga Broumas, says:[7]

Everyone should consider disappearing for a while into another voice! . . . In allowing someone else into my work, I realized that composition was more dynamic than I'd thought before, and that what was sacred about language, for me, was not so much its genesis as its transformation. . . . I hesitate to admit that collaboration is the place where I began to trust myself as a writer, but in fact, at least part of the confidence I have comes from trusting the creation of a third participant, the "us," which, in turn, led me to recognize the many selves who compose my work. When I lived in my imagination, I held vainly to a code about creation: that it took place in a silence that was private. Animating one's privacy with another person's magic was something beyond me until Olga persuaded me that there was nothing to lose. Indeed! Art is stubborn, and says what it has to say.

Taking our cue from the pleasure we felt reading David Shapiro's collaborative poems, Stephen Paul Miller (a contributor to this volume) and I attempted our own collaboration to honor the spirit of Shapiro's work. We wrote the following poem two words at a time, each of the two words having to contain D, J, and S, David's full initials. We attempted to do what Carl Withaus says Shapiro does: "traces words over and over until from within his effort to foreground the material of linguistic signs, narrative (of sorts) emerges."[8]

David Joel Shapiro

Disk jockeys spin déjà vu
jiffy-popping sadistic song.
David enjoys just doing judo kicks,
discursively projecting
"je ne sais quoi" decasyllabics.
His jurisdiction reaches Jordan,
adjacent to the stadium
of Taj Dispondee.
Jaded job-related sedated doubts
justify Jewish dating.
Janitors dodge Jesus's dandruff
then jump shards of dejected skylight.

Lumberjacks denounce the jasmine dew.
Judge Judy's jackass dies.
Jazz devotees skyjack Hadassah.
Mojo divas drink juice and soda.
St. John, the disciple of Jackson 5's
"Dancing Machine," adjusts his thong,
and jiggles John the Baptist's donut.
Claims adjusters jilt dozens of jumbo debutantes
and junior diamondbacks. David's ejector-seat

spreads joy to Jacksonville. Dogs jam
to the Judd sisters. Jag mediums
muddle jigsaw-shaded jaguars
who jumpstart Dodge Darts. Dad's in La Jolla
hijacking oldies, subject to ludicrous days in jail.
The Adventures of Joaquín Dubois (the Jester)
majorities fundamentalism and progressive jargon.
John Conyers decides Detroit's Jack and Jill
jigger pseudo-elections.

Notes

1. Elizabeth Bassford, "The Beautiful View: Lunch with David Shapiro," *Exoterica.* (2003) *http://www.exoterica.org/shapirointerview.html*.

2. Thomas Fink, "David Shapiro's "Possibilist Poetry,' " *Jacket 24.* (November 2003) *http://jacketmagazine.com/24.html.*

3. Joanna Fuhrman, "Pluralist Music: An Interview with David Shapiro," *Rain Taxi Online.* (Fall 2002) http://www.raintaxi.com/online/2002fall/shapiro.shtml.

4. Carl Whithaus, "Immediate Memories: (Nostalgic) Time and (Immediate) Loss in the Poetry of David Shapiro," *Rocky Mountain Language Association.* (1997) *http://rmmla.wsu.edu/ereview/53.1/articles/Whithaus/asp.*

5. Richard Hell and David Shapiro. "IV," *Richard Hell: Official Site.* (2003) *www.richardhell.com/IVpoem.html*.

6. Ibid.

7. Jocelyn Emerson, "An Interview with Jane Miller," *Electronic Poetry Review,* Issue 1 (2002) *http://www.poetry.org/issues/issue1/alltext/intmil.htm.*

8. Whithaus, "Immediate Memories. . . ."

Written and Rewritten to Order: The Gift of Generative Possibility in the Work of David Shapiro

Noah Eli Gordon

WHETHER IN INTERVIEWS, ESSAYS, MONOGRAPHS ON ARTISTS AND poets, or even his own poetry, David Shapiro always displays an active and elucidating generosity, one which consistently foregrounds the importance and influence of other working artists on his own writing. Regrettably, the past scarcity of scholarship on his work demonstrates how rarified such attention to generosity can be. In many ways Shapiro is a transitional figure who, because he arose on the cusp of extreme specialization in the arts, moving freely between the now ghettoized worlds of art criticism and poetry, was never entirely given his due by either. Granted, there are exceptions, an examination of the implications for two of which shall follow. Poets Michael Palmer and Peter Gizzi have both published works that are in conversation with the poetry of David Shapiro. Palmer's ancillary association with Language writing and current influential status among practitioners of innovative or experimental poetries, combined with Gizzi's dedication to community building, as a teacher, an editor, and a writer with ranging appeal, testify to the extensive influence of Shapiro's poetry.

Shapiro's "Music Written to Order" opens with an oscillatory gesture, a recreation of the fluctuating temporal conditions, rather than a severing of time into infinite present and irretrievable past. Attentive to the little words, specifically to the powerfully pluralist conjunction "and," Shapiro enacts poetic simultaneity: "Now and then, now and then, now and then" (*L*). The severing takes place in the following line, where the addition of the suffix "ness" to both versatile parts of speech morphs the previously unifying conjunctions into a guillotine-like device of difference: "Now-ness and then-ness." Shapiro goes on to erect, between the divided states, a field upon which the poem is able to play out its intimate address to the second person: "And between now and then / You hear the sound of a projector / And revisit your ancient home, your new home of late."

There is an ambiguity to Shapiro's "projector". One can read the entirety of the poem after such a line as the representation of a film, albeit a film built from the quick juxtapositions and image-heavy canon of filmmakers like Chris Marker or Stan Brakhage. Alternately, Shapiro's poem, like the work of Marker and Brakhage, allows for a nonlinear reading, its constituent phrases accruing an ambient meaning via their accumulation.[1]

There is a different sort of film being shown in Michael Palmer's "Music Rewritten," which features the parenthetical acknowledgement underneath its title: "*after D.S.*" Thus, Palmer's poem, as a rewriting of Shapiro's "Music Written to Order," becomes an example of what Shapiro himself, in his book on John Ashbery, advocated: "[P]oetry can no longer rely on simple releasing speech, but must rely on the most complex *re-writing* of releasing speech."[2] Palmer's poem begins with an oscillation similar to Shapiro's; however, here the sense of time is given complexity through its roots in affirmation and negation: "Yes and no then yes and no / Soon there'll be time enough for you."[3] The poem continues by recounting in near clinical terms what appear to be scenes from a pornographic film:[4]

> Charlie has swallowed the fluid
> L has come inside a box
>
> which some people paid to watch
> Yes and no yes and no

Although Palmer's rewrite has replaced the reverent nostalgia of Shapiro's original with a decidedly more ominous and distanced atmosphere, the simple act of rewriting is tantamount to an acknowledgment of the value of Shapiro's work. Such a gesture may even be considered a form of latent supplication. Philosopher Alphonso Lingis, in an essay on communication entitled "The Murmur of the World" writes, "To address a query or even a greeting to another is to expose one's ignorance, one's lacks, and one's destitution and is to appeal for assistance to one non-symmetrical with oneself."[5] Overlooking the pejorative implications of "non-symmetrical," Lingis's statement, applied to the communicative act of poetry, carries with it the color of one appealing to the Muse for inspiration. Among the implications of such an appeal is its ability to serve as a gesture of authenticity. To rewrite the poem of another is to elevate the other's poem to a place of import, anointing it with the status of an original, whose presence, according to Walter Benjamin, "is the prerequisite to the concept of authenticity."[6] Thus, Palmer's inclusion of "*after D.S.*," cryptic as it may be, educes both the legitimacy and generative possibility of the poetry of David Shapiro.

This gesture of invocation on the part of Palmer is something of a gift. "An essential portion of any artist's labor," according to Lewis Hyde, in his book *The Gift: Imagination and the Erotic Life of Property*, "is not creation so much as invocation. Part of the work cannot be made, it must be received; and we cannot have this gift except, perhaps, by supplication, by courting, by creating within ourselves that 'begging bowl' to which the gift is drawn."[7] Hyde's work on the notion of the Gift, although rooted in Marcel Mauss's anthropological writings, veers away from any sense of expected reciprocity, wherein gift exchange functions to solidify social and economic relations. For Hyde, "it is true that something often comes back when a gift is given, but if this were made an explicit condition of exchange, it wouldn't be a gift."[8] Georges Bataille has argued that inherent to giving is the acquisition for the giver of a heightened status from the receiver. "[T]he gift," he writes, "would be senseless (and so we would never decide to give) if it did not take on the meaning of an acquisition. Hence *giving* must become *acquiring of power*."[9] Hyde moves consideration of the gift outside of the framework of economic exchange and toward the more ambiguous sphere of artistic labor and its attendant life of the imagination. It is here that power is made manifest in the more difficultly measured sense of cultural, rather than economic, capital.

However, to consider Palmer's gift to Shapiro as one tinged merely with self-interest would be to read his gesture as something other than the celebratory occasion that it is. As Simone Weil, writing on friendship, states, "There is no contradiction between seeking our own good in a human being and wishing for his good to be increased."[10] Shapiro, himself a practitioner of the "allusion," "quote," and "appropriation"[11] has noted, in an interview with Joanna Fuhrman:[12]

The saddest thing in poetry is where you have what I regard as male competition. Neo-Nietzschean noble rivalry is one thing, but it becomes very male, in which one person wins and one loses. Tennis: which is not poetry. Then there's the Swedenborgian "the more angles the more room." Meyer Schapiro, if he praised Jackson Pollock, would praise someone doing an equal and opposite kind of work. He liked the underdog. Sometimes I think there's an irresponsibility which certain scientists know—if a scientist doesn't footnote a work on penicillin it's considered a lack of generosity. Meyer Schapiro said the love of footnotes was a love of generosity.

Palmer's "*after D.S.*" is analogous to the act of footnoting. The generosity implicit in the inclusion of the footnote serves a dual function: the announcement of merit, viability, and importance of the already existent work and the imperative to seek out that work. Palmer, asked about the use of quotation in his own writing, responded:[13]

> I like the possibility of intertextuality. I am a reader, perhaps too much of one, and I live to some degree in the book. *I like the possibility of bringing in other people's words* to reflect the fact that for me experience flows at all levels, whether it's hearing a car out the window or *reading something that is affecting me profoundly*. Reading becomes co-extensive with the other experiences in my life, and it enters the poem like any other object or experience. It becomes a kind of layering of the text. *Maybe it is also a directive to people to go out and look* at that in the way that a lot of the stuff Pound threw into *The Cantos* was to get people to read a wonderful Chinese or Provencal poet. So the poem becomes then a shared place among a variety of texts, without, I hope, ever becoming simply a collage.

The notion of the copy is a central trope for Shapiro: the first line of his latest book, *A Burning Interior*, reads: "of a copy of nothing" (1); *After a Lost Original*, whose title immediately anchors the book to Shapiro's ongoing investigation of the trope, begins with the line: "When the translation and the original meet" (11); the title poem of *To An Idea* contains in its penultimate line the almost sardonically delivered: "as if copying could exist" (15); *House (Blown Apart)*, also beginning with its title poem, contains the lines: "Old work we might parody as an homage / Losing after all the very idea of parody" (15), a nearly perfect copy or echo (and thus a perfected enactment) of a phrase from Shapiro's earlier writing on Ashbery: "[I]t is to parody most that Ashbery turns in his later works, if only to annihilate by its total use the very idea of parody"[14]; "Needed Inventions," an early poem in *Lateness*, laments: "The problem of the firefly / Is such a delicate one / If we could only copy the firefly exactly / This problem might be done."

Discussing Meyer Schapiro's essay on Cézanne, David Shapiro writes: "Schapiro restores our sense that an artist is deeply invested in his usual constellation of images."[15] Such a constellation for Shapiro includes, among other things: snow, knives, venetian blinds, clouds, violins, the page, photographs, golf balls and billiard balls, insects, airplanes, and, of course, the above mentioned copy, with all of its ancillary lexicon: trace, parody, shadow, original, outline, rewrite, correction fluid, and so on. Shapiro gives a heightened level of attention to the plasticity of his imagery. The opening line of his poem titled, simply, "A Wall," reads: "I have the right not to represent it" (*HBA* 24). The nuance of humor and depth present in much of his work, combined with a subject matter that is often laced to the problem of what, exactly, constitutes one's subject, allows for an open-ended reading, a reading which revolves around the generative possibility of remaining engaged with the multiple levels of each poem, or, for the poet-reader, reimagining the work as what Shapiro has called Stein's *Stanzas in Meditation*: "[A] powerful source book."[16]

One such reader who has harnessed the sense of possibility in Shapiro's work is Peter Gizzi. Asked about his reading practice in a 1993 interview, he responded:[17]

> No matter what book I read, it is my book. Every painting I look at becomes my painting. At some level of the reading. It doesn't stay there, it doesn't begin there. But at some level of the exchange it is mine. Some way into the process it becomes other once again, but parts of it are left in me. Parts of the cadences, the phrases, the vocabulary. The particular histories that it rehearses. The events emotional, historical, social. Some of that remains in me. It helps articulate me.

This process of embodying outside texts, of including that which is "other" in order to articulate one's self, is expounded by Alphonso Lingis, who writes: "One enters into conversation in order to become an other for the others."[18] The implication here is similar to that of the footnote. By attesting to the existence of a source text with which one is in conversation, one is simultaneously attesting to the importance of the source and to one's own work in relation to it. The notes page that closes Gizzi's collection *Artificial Heart* is replete with mention of the work of others with whom Gizzi is in conversation. Concerning his poem "Rewriting the Other and the Others," he explains: "As an attempt to erase a work, à la Rauschenburg & de Kooning, *Rewriting the Other and the Others* is an 'erasure' of the poem 'The Other and the Others' by David Shapiro."[19]

Just as Rauschenberg's decision to erase a work of de Kooning's invariably asserts the legitimacy of de Kooning's importance to the younger artist, so Gizzi's "erasure" of Shapiro's "The Other and the Others" carries the same reverential testimony. And such testimony in effect becomes a work of art in and of itself. Shapiro, in an anti-Bloomian dictum within his book on Ashbery, writes: "The poem and the relations between poems must become a matter of the joys of influence. The best poetry of our day is, more over, a form of literary criticism, both in drab and golden tones."[20]

Shapiro's "The Other and the Others," from his 1983 collection, *To An Idea*, begins:

> I wanted to paint the night sky
> Too easy to make a black xerox
>
> You are Persephone with a torch
> In you the slenderness of the end of the century.
>   (89)

The simplicity of Shapiro's diction, while immediate and uncomplicated, reveals one of his trademark strengths as a poet. Although this is uniformly referential writing, there is a sense of uncertainty, or, more poignantly, of numerous certainties, as to the mimetic qualities here. One is able to read even in the first line variant meanings. Is it the desire to create a representation of the night sky using paint? Is it an admission of the ambition one harbors in desiring to enter the pantheon of creation myths, becoming the one who gives to the sky its blackness? Shapiro's poems carry with them openness as regards his relationship with mimeses. As often as reality is reproduced—as opposed to being merely represented—it is replaced with associative dream logic or evocative allusion. The second couplet here, in which the address turns toward both the second person and Greek mythology, exemplifies such strategies.

From pottery to ancient coinage, Persephone is often depicted holding a torch, although such depictions are representative of the period immediately following her initial rescue by Demeter. More common is the depiction of Demeter as torchbearer, frantically searching for her daughter. The torch, when appearing in Persephone's arms, is indicative of her comfort in her role as part-time queen of the underworld, a symbol of one's acceptance of power. Undoubtedly, Persephone would have such a torch in hand when making her infamous bargain with Orpheus. As with his diction, the strength of Shapiro's allusion is its ability to allow for multiple reading. It's not ambiguous as much as it is multifarious, evoking a discursive set of emotive states, whether that of bewilderment or of near tyrannical megalomania.

It is therefore difficult to attempt a rewrite of this poem. In doing so, one inevitably selects a specific reading, casting aside alternatives, regardless of how applicable they may be. Unlike Palmer's poem, which appropriates some of the linguistic constructions of the Shapiro poem, specifically the opening of a third allusive condition between two already existent states, Gizzi's rewrite is, in the words of Shapiro's poem "Two-Four Time": "[A]lways the same word-for-word translation" (*PT* 25). Gizzi's "erasure" begins:[21]

> I wanted to model the morning light
> Too difficult to impasto the sky
>
> You are Alcestis with a kite
> The years whip by and tears cover answers.

"Rewriting the Other and the Others" maintains the couplet form and syntax of its source, while replacing certain parts of speech with their opposite, and others with either an alternative word choice or an entirely different phrase, allowing Gizzi's poem the effect of maintaining "[p]arts of the cadences, the phrases, the vocabulary" of the original. Where the torch that Shapiro has given Persephone might bring light to the underworld, the kite with which Gizzi equips Alcestis is a celebration of her having returned from it. In this way, Gizzi's "erasure" becomes the "black xerox" of Shapiro's poem, a photographic negative vouching for the original's authenticity. Shapiro ends his poem with the following lines: "To enter Liberty's body, a copy of a copy! / As a noiseless plane, a worm, dove into its casket" (*TI* 89). And Gizzi's rewrite ends: "Then reverse the Tyrants' ideology, an original of an original! / And a noisy sphere, a bird strafes air."[22]

By transforming "a copy of a copy" into "an original of an original," "[t]he Tyrants' ideology" here can be read as a playful, yet reverent, parody of Shapiro himself. Gizzi celebrates perhaps the brightest star in Shapiro's constellation of images, the copy, and in doing so demonstrates the reception of the gift of Shapiro's work, which culminates in the reproduction of what Hyde calls "the gifted state"—an embodying of one's imaginative spirit within an actual work—as evinced through the existence of Gizzi's own poem.[23] Yet Shapiro also is attuned to the mutability of his writing. His poem "Write Out," from *House (Blown Apart)*, published five years after *To An Idea*, begins with the following stanza:

> I wanted to paint the night sky
> So I considered a black Xerox
> and my medium was correction pen fluid
> the blue correction formerly too dry to work.
>
> (49)

This is an obvious rewrite of elements of "The Other and the Others," and a subtle echo of the poem "The Night Sky," from Shapiro's 1973 collection, *The Page-Turner*. Shapiro is a poet for whom the materials of production are consistently laid bare. His poetry occupies a place of becoming, rather than merely being, as one is, in reading his work, often located on the satisfyingly generative field between the imaginative impulse and its manifestation as an actual artifact. Take, for example, the opening stanza of "The Sphinx, Again":

> To keep photographing the same ice
> In the same river flowing beneath the same bridge
> Tying to link the shadow of a word to another word
> Staring into the same sign of signs for nothing.
>
> (*HBA* 48)

Or the first stanza of "An Example of Work":

> The bluejay is bobbing out in the yard, as if amusing itself
>   with a country dance
> That is a line you say that will produce guffaws in the Church
> Well, first I saw a phrase in the dictionary *amusing herself*
>   *with a the contredanse*
> And then I wanted to use the verb "bobbing."
>
> (*TI* 46)

Or the opening to "House of the Secret":

> I met the old dead poet
> And told him I no longer loved my work
> As I had when a child or even fifteen
> Sorry I had not written someone else's poem but it was already
>   written.
>
> (*ALO* 21)

Or, finally, the first two lines from "Drawing After Summer," which echo the poem "Summer," appearing seven pages earlier in *After a Lost Original*: "I saw the ruins of poetry, of a poetry / Of a parody and it was a late copy bright as candy" (88).

Everywhere in Shapiro's poetry one finds the tracings of a crossover between the imagination and the work it might (and ultimately, does) produce. In many ways, the tracing is simply a reconstruction of the myriad frustrations of one's inability ever to completely realize the transition, enabling his work to remain in flux, to enact the gifted state. Both Palmer and Gizzi share with Shapiro this anxiety of the finality of representation. Palmer's "Music Rewritten" ends:[24]

> First there's sameness then difference
> then the letter X across a face
>
> then a line through a name
> which is the wrong name in any case.

And Gizzi's recent work has included this totemic line: "I am far and I am an animal and I am just another I-am poem, a we-see poem, a they-love poem."[25] Both Palmer and Gizzi, in making use of the work of David Shapiro, in celebrating and honoring it, have fulfilled what Lewis Hyde considers an essential element of the gift—its continued transference.

Notes

1. David Shapiro, commenting on Rimbaud, has touted the value of such an approach: "The sentences are held paratactically, with the sternest breakdown of connectives. This expunging of the connective tissue holds the widest possibilities for painting, music, and poetry" (*Poets and Painters* 11).

2. David Shapiro, *John Ashbery: An Introduction to the Poetry* (New York: Columbia University Press, 1979), 10.

3. Michael Palmer, *First Figure* (San Francisco: North Point, 1984), 35.
4. Ibid.
5. Alphonso Lingis, *The Community of Those Who Have Nothing in Common* (Bloomington and Indianapolis: Indiana University Press, 1994), 87.
6. Walter Benjamin, *Illuminations*, trans. Harry Zohn (New York: Schoken, 1969), 220.
7. Hyde, *The Gift: Imagination and the Erotic Life of Property* (New York: Vintage Books, 1983), 144.
8. Ibid., 9.
9. Quoted in David Kosalka, "Georges Bataille and the Notion of Gift." 1999. *The Historian Underground.* <http://www.lemmingland.com/bataille.html>
10. Simone Weill, *The Simone Weil Reader*, ed. George A. Panichas. (Mt. Kisco, NY: Moyer Bell Limited, 1977), 367.
11. David Shapiro, "After the New York School." Interview with Joseph Lease. *Pataphysics Magazine.* 1990. <http://www.pataphysicsmagazine.com/shapiro_interview.html> For a valuable discussion of Shapiro's rewriting of a poem by Yeats, see "After A Lost Original: David Shapiro" by Chris Stroffolino, reprinted in his collection of essays, *Spin Cycle.*
12. David Shapiro, "Pluralist Music: An Interview with David Shapiro." Interview with Joanna Fuhrman. *Rain Taxi.* Fall 2002. 15 Sep. 2005. <http://www.raintaxi.com/online/2002fall/shapiro.shtml>
13. Michael Palmer, in Lee Bartlett, *Talking Poetry: Conversations in the Workshop with Contemporary Poets* (Albuquerque: University of New Mexico Press, 1987), 138–39. (my emphasis)
14. David Shapiro, *John Ashbery: An Introduction to the Poetry*, 79.
15. David Shapiro, "Mondrian's Secret." In *Uncontrollable Beauty*, ed. Bill Beckley with David Shapiro (New York: Allworth Press, 1998), 309.
16. David Shapiro, *Poets and Painters: Lines of Color* (Denver: Denver Art Museum, 1979), 13.
17. Peter Gizzi, Interview with Samuel Truitt. 1993. Brown University. http://www.brown.edu/Departments/Literary_Arts/pgizzitruitt.html>
18. Alphonso Lingis, 88.
19. Peter Gizzi, "Notes." *Artificial Heart* (Providence: Burning Deck, 1998).
20. David Shapiro, *John Ashbery: An Introduction to the Poetry*, 4.
21. Peter Gizzi, *Artificial Heart*, 76.
22. Ibid., 77.
23. Lewis Hyde, 151.
24. Michael Palmer, *First Figure*, 36.
25. Peter Gizzi, *Some Values of Landscape and Weather* (Middletown, CT: Wesleyan University Press, 2003), 81.

Shapiro's "A Man Holding an Acoustic Panel"

Ron Silliman

I ALMOST NEVER THINK OF DAVID SHAPIRO AS A NEW YORK SCHOOL poet. Like, say, Peter Schjeldahl, Shapiro has never been associated with any other literary tendency in his career, but seems so thoroughly independent that to characterize him as part of a larger collective impulse seems somehow inaccurate. Yet, as Shapiro would be the first to remind me, that is something of a faulty logic—I could probably theorize out every second-generation New York School poet save Ron Padgett and Joe Brainard (who themselves are no less independent, but rather sit at or near that rubric's bull's eye). Indeed, Shapiro coedited with Padgett the quasi-definitive 1970 Random House collection, *An Anthology of New York Poets*.[1]

The reason I was thinking of David Shapiro was the onset of George W. Bush's war, the death of a young woman under a bulldozer in the Gaza strip, and comments, implications more than statements, that were made on this blog last October and November that suggested that New York School poetry was generally apolitical. Thus I had suggested then that there were aspects of Louis Cabri's *The Mood Embosser* that could be read as Ted Berrigan + politics. That of course is too easy and flippant an approach to the question. So I went back and reread the title poem of *A Man Holding an Acoustic Panel*, a book published by E.P. Dutton in 1971. Now I have to take it all back.

It is important to keep in mind just how remarkable a book such as this was. Shapiro was born in 1947 and is thus one year younger than I. 1971 was the year I published my first book, *Crow*, with Ithaca House, a cooperative run by grad students in the writing program at Cornell.[2] It was also the year in which Alice Notley, born in 1945, published her first chapbook, *165 Meeting House Lane*. Published that same year, *A Man Holding an Acoustic Panel* was David Shapiro's *third* volume of poetry from a major New York trade publisher. His first book, *January*, came out with Holt when Shapiro was just 18; his second, *Poems from Deal*, from Dutton in 1969. *Panel* was short-listed for the 1972 National Book Award.[3] Shapiro had received Merrill Foundation and Book-of-the-Month Club grants, the Robert Frost Fellowship from Breadloaf, something called the New York Poets Award, and the *Kellett* Fellowship to Clare College, Cambridge. If this was not enough absolute star power, Shapiro had been sufficiently active in the 1968 student revolt at Columbia to have, in one action, occupied the president's office and gotten his photograph—feet on the desk and, if I remember correctly, with cigar—published as a full page spread in *Life* magazine. In his spare time, David Shapiro was a professional violinist. Not bad for a guy who started 1971 at the ripe old age of 23.[4]

This context is worth noting, because it is the one in which Shapiro's work was read by poets at some distance from New York. It was a context in which it was easier to remember the photo in *Life*, harder to recall that it had been taken in the midst of what was an illegal activity that entailed personal risk as well as a political conscience. Similarly, I think it was possible, even plausible, in 1971, to read "A Man Holding an Acoustic Panel," a suite contained of eighteen shorter poems, without recognizing it for the political poem it is. Let me turn that around just for emphasis—half of David Shapiro's third book is given over to a single long poem that is decidedly political, but readers may not have noticed. Certainly in far away Berkeley, where Free Speech Movement veterans tended to look at an organization like SDS, the pivotal group behind the Columbia strike, as a bunch of Johnnies-come-lately, the politics of "Acoustic Panel" proved not to be self evident.

The suite itself consists of eighteen poems, only one of which extends as far as three pages, in a wide range of styles—so great that any specific section, singled out, would probably misrepresent the whole. Shapiro can be extraordinarily lyrical at moments and yet also uses prose here in ways that extend the possibilities of prose, really for the first time in poetry since the Williams of *Kora* or Stein's *Tender Buttons*. Thus "The Danube Loophole" reads:

> On the ship there is an international airport.
> Here, their passports are taken away from them.
>
> These walls, these acoustical bricks, protect the man holding an acoustic panel against a wave of shock and sound.
>
> Ordinary microphones don't hear it, only the microphones with "great surface" permit us to—Walls and closets will not stop it—we will take these sounds to our grave.
>
> Hearts working with determined frequency like twenty hearts, hands black as glands.
>
> The heart contracts to the accompaniment of electric phenomena. Here is a microelectrode penetrating into the heart of a dog.
>
> <div align="right">(<i>MHAP</i> 11)</div>

The allusion to Williams in that last sentence is no coincidence. Nor is the couplet that leads off the poem—this is, at one level, a tale of coming to America. The presence of the work's overall title, indeed the book's title, points us directly to what this is all about: *a wave of shock and sound*. I am not clear on which loophole Shapiro might have in mind here—the Danube stretches from the Ukraine to the Black Sea, running through what are now eleven countries—the number fluctuates over time—and a search on Google turns up literally hundreds of possibilities.

But if there is a tale, there is not a plot. Here is the fourth section, "Statue of a Breeze on Horseback," just for the sake of contrast:

> In a corner of air
> On a couch built of air
> We make a very little angle
> Between "diode and triode lie near together
>
> Are you in the corner of meteors?
> You're in the crust of the earth
> You have not yet extinguished the light complex in me
> On my languorous couch of air
>
> Air, which is alternately
> Black and brilliant and crushed like a coin
> That lies under the rocks at Deal
> Normal as a neighbor and more clear

> You are here
> Here is the debut of culture
> Here is your light face which Michelson and Morley followed
> Here are the spores." Sir Alexander Fleming.
>
> (*MHAP* 14)

Note how those quotation marks work. Note also how Michelson and Morley take us right back to the question of waves from the first poem. But how radically differently this poem feels to be set into quatrains—how much of that determines what we feel about "You" and/or vice versa? And how, or why, does it lead to the inventor of penicillin? One could do a whole little riff of the sonic effects as well, following, for example, the ten instances of a hard *c* in this poem, nine of which start off words.

It seems clear to me that one cannot sketch out the eighteen works into an argument, as such—that is not their relation. Yet the ways in which these poems invoke history, as well as discourses such as science, make it instantly evident that the social realm *is* what is at stake—that for me is an almost perfect invocation of the political. Yet it is not the one-dimensional landscape one associates with a Levertov or Ferlinghetti. There is, for example, a running theme in these poems of small creatures: crickets, bees, squirrels, mice—as if Shapiro were anticipating the graphic fiction of Art Spiegelman.

The one overtly political poem in the sequence is "The Funeral of Jan Palach." Jan Palach was a twenty-year-old philosophy student who, in 1969, set himself ablaze in Prague to protest the Stalinoid depredations of the Soviet occupation of what was then Czechoslovakia. In dying, Palach became a profound symbol for the Czechoslovakian people and has become a permanent part of the folklore of his nation.[5] All that makes this poem not just political, but overt, lies entirely in its title. The poem itself directly addresses grief:

> When I entered the first meditation,
>   I escaped the gravity of the object,
> I experienced the emptiness,
>   And I have been dead a long time.
>
> When I had a voice you could call a voice,
>   My mother wept to me:
> My son, my beloved son,
>   I never thought this possible.

> I'll follow you on foot.
>   Halfway in mud and slush the microphones picked up.
> It was raining on the houses;
>   It was snowing on the police-cars.
>
> The astronauts were weeping,
>   Going neither up nor out.
> And my own mother was brave enough she looked
>   And it was all right I was dead.
>
> <div align="right">(<i>MHAP</i> 30)</div>

Even the lines that do not grammatically require end stops have some sort of punctuation right up to that next-to-last line, Shapiro controlling the reader's breathing and sense of halting rhythm, and again, the question of the microphones, which throughout this work is the question of empathy, which means both compassion and the ability to experience pain.

"A Man Holding an Acoustic Panel" is a dark and brooding work composed within a genre that has never been known for its seriousness. I have no idea how it was received by those close to Shapiro, but I know that at the time, my own response was incomprehension—I simply did not have the critical framework in my head at the time to *recognize* this work for what it was, and is. In an excellent interview conducted by Joanna Fuhrman for RainTaxi, David Shapiro brooded on a comment Marianne Moore once made about his work lacking "adequate starkness." There is hardly anything inadequate about the starkness here. Shapiro's poem, as it turned out, inspired architect John Hejduk's monument to Palach in Prague. So it is no accident, I suppose, that I have been thinking about this poem this week, not only in the context of the tragedy of Iraq, but also the homicide of Rachel Corrie, the 23-year-old Olympia, Washington native who was literally bulldozed to death by the Israeli army last weekend. Unlike Palach and his American and Vietnamese counterparts in the 1960s, Corrie did not plan her fate. In the wake of the media overload over Iraq, I worry that her sacrifice will disappear from our memories if we ever even take note of it in the first place. But I'm glad to note that it's possible to write political poetry from within the framework of the New York School. It is possible even to write great political poetry there—David Shapiro has shown us how.[6]

Notes

1. David Shapiro and Ron Padgett, Eds., *An Anthology of New York Poets* (New York: Random, 1970). This is a volume that includes not just the usual suspects, but others whose connection may seem more tenuous to the aesthetics of founding papas Ashbery, O'Hara, Koch, and Schuyler—John Giorno, Ed Sanders, Tom Veitch—and whose introduction mumbles an apology for failing to include Allen Ginsberg and Charles Reznikoff, but remains silent over its inclusion of only a single woman, Bernadette Mayer. No Waldman, no Notley, no Guest, all of whom would have been reasonable inclusions in 1970.

2. Ithaca House was a funky little operation, funded by a writing professor, Baxter Hathaway, as a means of instructing students in what the poetry world was really like. Because David McAleavey had, then getting his PhD there, written what I think might have been the first dissertation on George Oppen, Ithaca House in the early 1970s published first books by David Melnick and Bob Perelman, as well as Ray *Di* Palma's second volume.

3. Frank O'Hara and Howard Moss were awarded the prize that year, O'Hara posthumously.

4. New York trade publishers were quite open to New York poets up to a certain moment in time—thus Lewis Mac Adams, Dick *Gallup*, Tom Clark, and Clark Coolidge all had early trade press books. I don't understand the landscape in that part of the publishing world well enough to know how, why, or even quite at what exact moment that all came to a crashing halt, but it certainly did. By 1975, the poets of St. Marks might as well have been back in Tulsa as far as the trades were concerned. Ashbery, Schuyler, and Koch would be the only ones to retain access to that level of distribution.

5. By contrast, the self-immolation of Norman Morrison, a Quaker father of three, in front of Robert McNamara's office at the Pentagon had less of an impact in the United States than it did in Vietnam, where he became a household name. The other Americans who committed such acts to protest the Vietnam War, Alice Herz, Roger LaPorte, and George Winne, at best became answers to trivia questions.

6. This essay was originally published on Ron Silliman's Blog, March 22, 2003, http://ronsilliman.blogspot.com/2003_03_01_ronsilliman_archive.html.

Uncanny Narrative in Shapiro's
A Burning Interior

Thomas Fink

IN THE EARLY 1970S, DAVID SHAPIRO CHOSE TO PAY PARTICULAR attention to the least narrative of the first generation New York School poets, John Ashbery, by writing the first doctoral dissertation on him. Ashbery had not yet won the three major prizes that *Self-Portrait in a Convex Mirror* earned him in 1975, and so one can imagine various Columbia University English professors—if not Kenneth Koch—skeptical of this project. Shapiro, in this 1974 text and in the 1979 revision, *John Ashbery: An Introduction to the Poetry*, published when he himself was an Assistant Professor in the Columbia English department, heavily emphasizes Ashbery's poetic critique of referentiality. Moreover, there is one telling reference to narrative in Shapiro's chapter on *The Tennis Court Oath*, Ashbery's most disjunctive work and a major influence on Language poets like Bruce Andrews: "While structurally the poems may vacillate, the Proust-like repetition of the elements never in a sense guarantees more than a vague impression of narrative, never rises toward the dangerous omen of a plot but gives *a taste of a plot*."[1] As Shapiro, in his reading of Ashbery, engages in a strong critique of conventional narrative modes, we sense from this passage, especially the phrase, "dangerous omen," that he is experiencing a productive ambivalence about the future of narrative.

Various passages in the Ashbery book demonstrate that Shapiro, like the Language poets but unlike the senior New York School poets, read much poststructuralist theory in the seventies—for example, in his Derridean notions of centering and decentering, approving reference to Paul de Man, and mention of "a Lacanian sense . . . of endless narcissistic possibility and impossibility"[2] in the long poem "Self-Portrait in a Convex Mirror." A great deal of this theory, of course, continually and severely puts the traditional coherence of narrative modes in question, and Shapiro's affirmation of this aspect of poststructuralist critique dovetails with his admiration of such figures as Mallarmé, Stein, and even the "collagistic" T.S. Eliot of *The Waste Land*, as well as such contemporaries as Clark Coolidge and Joseph Ceravolo. Further, Shapiro's strong interest in innovative visual art (including Jasper Johns, about whom he would publish a book in 1984, and Robert Rauschenberg), music (John Cage, Eliot Carter, and Laurie Anderson), and theater (Robert Wilson) encouraged the tendency to be skeptical about narrative.[3] Shapiro's highly disjunctive poetry of this period and before—ranging from poems like "The Heavenly Humor" in *Poems from Deal* (1969) to "The Devil's Trill Sonata," the long poem in *Lateness* (1977) —can be said to enact or embody such rigorous questioning.

At St. Marks Church, a New York School gathering place in the East Village of Manhattan, Shapiro undoubtedly interacted in the seventies with some of the east coast poets who were central to the development of Language writing, but he was not affiliated with them in any significant way. One prominent feature of seventies Language poetry, of course, is an anti-narrative stance that seems much more thorough-going than, say, any such tendency in the New York School. In a collection of statements of poetics by six Language poets "for *Change*" anthologized in Ron Silliman's 1986 anthology, *In the American Tree*, Bob Perelman offers a possible justification for the proscription of narrative:[4]

> This writing does not concern itself with narrative in the conventional sense. Story, plot, any action outside the syntactic and tonal actions of the words is seen as secondary. Attempts to posit an idealized narrative time would only blur perception of the actual time of writing and reading. Persona, Personism, the poem as trace of the poet-demiurge—these, too, are now extraneous. The functions that narrative had fulfilled, those of creating and resolving tension, introducing material, motivating sequence, are now dealt with more directly by a variety of procedures. . . . Specific areas of vocabulary and syntax, or modes of patterning will be investigated.

Perelman goes on to state that "narrative-like elements do arise naturally," from the work of such poets as Clark Coolidge, Ron Silliman, Lyn Hejinian, Charles Bernstein, and Steve Benson, but, for him, the presence of these elements does not constitute narrative.

Nevertheless, he admits that "Carla Harryman's work" frequently features a discernible "narrative . . . , though it will be refracted and redefined by her language's self-scrutiny." In other words, he and the Language poets find "direct investigations of narrative" in the process of composing narrative much more acceptable than narrative that lacks self-reflexivity. Also valorizing the disfiguration of narrative, Perelman adds that "in some works" he himself "has presented strings of narrative device without matching narrative content," and Peter Seaton sometimes allows "the ghost of a narrative" to linger, "not quite effaced by other signal-noise."

While Perelman's formulations seem to advocate "investigation" that "redefines narrative"[5] rather than forbids it to practitioners, it is a matter of historical record that many poets who have come in significant contact with Language Poetry in the last thirty years perceive the emphasis on disjunction as, in practical terms, elimination of narrative as a possibility. In his retrospective "Long Note on New Narrative" in *Narrativity* (undated, but probably in the late nineties), California poet Robert Gluck, a self-styled "fellow traveler" of the Language poets in the seventies and early eighties, reports that, on the one hand, he "experienced the poetry of disjunction as a luxurious idealism in which the speaking subject rejects the confines of representation and disappears in the largest freedom, language itself," but on the other hand, this was unsatisfactory, because "political agency" for him as a gay man "involved at least a provisionally stable identity" to counter the "tyranny" of mainstream representation of gays.[6] Thus, he, Bruce Boone, Kevin Killian, Dodie Bellamy, and others posited "the New Narrative"—"a hybrid aesthetic, something impure"—as a way of making narrative a viable part of poetic experimentation: "We (eventually we were gay, lesbian, and working class writers) could not let narration go."[7] Gluck declares:[8]

> I wanted to write with a total continuity and total disjunction since I experienced the world (and myself) as continuous and infinitely divided. . . . Why should a work of literature be organized by one pattern of engagement? Why should a "position" be maintained regarding the size of the gaps between units of meaning? . . . . I wanted the pleasures and politics of the fragment and the pleasures and politics of story, gossip, fable, and case history; the randomness of chance and a sense of inevitability; sincerity while using appropriation and pastiche.

Even if many of those who embraced this "New Narrative" perspective chose to write novels, the (re-)inclusion of narrative in poetry is central to Gluck's analysis.

Gluck's preoccupations with proscription are revisited, with differences, by Mark Wallace, speaking for the poets of a younger generation, in his 1998 account of "Language and Postlanguage Poetries" in *Flashpoint*. Acknowledging Language Poetry's extensive, if not hegemonic, influence on younger U.S. experimental poets with the term "postlanguage," Wallace asserts that "postlanguage poets have accepted" theoretical formulations posited by Language poets in the seventies and eighties—for example, "that language structures inevitably affect, and are affected by, the politics of cultural production," "that language is constructed by relations of power, and that it cannot naively access either transcendence or the natural world, or unproblematically represent the way the world 'actually is.'"[9] However, he asserts that those he identifies as "postlanguage poets" often decide to ignore such proscription, "to use "narrative, lyric, spirituality, and a poetics of the everyday" consciously, "without returning to the sort of naïve justifications of those elements that continue to be a feature of more mainstream American poetry." What occurs from this is "the extension of key questions asked by the language poets into areas that the language poets were not interested in."[10]

David Shapiro has often pursued a questioning of narrative in the process of narrating—seldom straightforwardly—(within lyric meditation). "Redefining" narrative, this utilization of narrative goes well beyond conventional functions. In a 1990 interview with Joseph Lease, he declares, "I think if you're going to give up one form of storytelling you're going to have to do it another way,"[11] rather than suggesting that narrative should be banished altogether. I believe that young poets, critics, and general readers of poetry who would identify, at least to some degree, with concerns motivating Wallace's grouping of "postlanguage" would do well to avail themselves of the opportunity to examine Shapiro's uses of narrative in light of their own "key questions." Currently, journals like *Talisman* (and some Language poets themselves) are forcefully demonstrating that the landscape of contemporary innovative poetry is rife with filiations and affiliations that exceed the dominant presence of any one camp, and this could bring more focused attention to work like Shapiro's. "Postlanguage" and other young innovators can find in Shapiro a contemporary of the Language poets who has powerfully addressed "postlanguage" concerns independently of both the influence of seventies and eighties Language Poetry and their own affiliative networks. This is not to pit Shapiro's accomplishments against those of the Language Poets—some of whom (including Charles Bernstein and Bob Perelman), according to Wallace, "have" recently "been incorporating elements that might be thought of as postlanguage," including "narrative,"[12]—but to acknowledge the relevance of Shapiro's work in a new frame.

While salient examples can be drawn from each phase of Shapiro's career, my specimen texts will come from the poet's most recent book, *A Burning Interior* (2002). In "Winter Work," Shapiro risks and eludes sentimentality (and, given the drift of his poetics, narrative coherence) in considering the situation of a domestic animal:

> A dog prays.
>   For me.
> He barks inside all day, what little inside there is, like a pigeon.
> Help!
> He kneels for his king one night
> Kind owner. "Ayekah?" All is kind,
>   All is cruel.
> A dog's prayed, obeyed, spayed.
> In the forest now, he moans for help
> In some of his languages. No one!
> The addressee slips away,
> Has slipped away.
> But a dog thinks.
> The dog thanks you in the desert.
> In the desert
> Of the desert, you have left a trace.
>
> (*BI* 98)

A quick reading might establish that, apart from the skilful deployment of widely varying line-lengths, this is merely a cute story entailing praise for a creature who ceaselessly exhibits a touching loyalty and mild lamentation (or censure?) for its master's inability to return that devotion. But the opening lines register interesting tonal uncertainty: in attributing the formal expression of spiritual activity to a dog, is the poet trying to be serious or parodistic? Dogs supposedly "beg" when taught to do so, and "begging" may resemble "prayer," but the personification seems deliberately excessive. And the fragmentary second line offers ambiguity with great concision. One reading would indicate that the dog's "work" is the altruistic act of seeking spiritual salvation for its master, the poem's speaker, and the other would identify the dog's aim as securing the presence of the master for its own gratification.

The question of varying human perspectives on canine motivation or instinct in response to the environment grows even more apparent in the long third line; interiority can be literal or figurative. The dog may be physically confined in relatively "little" space "all day," or the "inside" could be an extremely limited subjectivity. The simile tacked on to the end of the line is another disruption of narrative movement. "A pigeon" does not "bark" but "squawks," and it is an outdoor bird, so the poet may be comparing the limited mental functioning of dogs to that of pigeons, *unless* he is trying to show that *this* dog has undergone such truncation of possibility that its bark has withered into a pigeon-like squawk.

The pun of "night" / "knight" may posit the dog as a strangely heroic supplicant of a "king" who comes home from work at night but is out of reach. "'Ayekah?'" means "Where are you?" (or perhaps, "Where art thou?") in Hebrew, also suggesting that the dog's search for the master's embrace is a spiritual quest, like a human being's longing for the felt presence of an absent god. The echo of the Shakespearean "cruel to be kind" in the paradoxical conflation of total cruelty and kindness is a narrative evaluation that encourages speculation rather than delivering insight. Does the dog, praying for contact with the master, imagine that he is entirely "kind" and loving, while the master is actually (though perhaps inadvertently) "cruel" in not being able to deliver? Is it an all or nothing situation? Or does the word "kind" serve as a shorthand for the Shakespearean "in kind" or typical—a typically cruel scenario?

Even if these questions are not answered, Shapiro's triple rhyme of past tense verbs renders a story of betrayal as concisely as possible: presumed to act intentionally and not merely instinctually, the dog takes two actions of ingratiation but is "rewarded" by becoming the passive victim of a third. Exiled "in the forest," the moaning creature seems to be posited as an object of pity, but once again, an odd phrase troubles narrative flow. Here, "moaning" is not distinguished from "barking" because the dog only "moans," not barks, "for help /

In [multiple] languages," but the poet does not tell us what these languages that express pain might be. How is the dog's "consciousness" or "psyche" divided? What analogy between a multilingual human being and a dog makes sense? Perhaps "the addressee" (the p[o]et owner or the reader of the poem) slips away" or "always already" "has slipped away," not because of indifference to a pet's affective needs, but because of bafflement about how to interpret the possible multiplicity of canine communication in a way that promotes mutual contentment. But the lines can also be read very differently: the human "addressee," in believing fantasies of communication based on personification—on the concept of a pet having a nonverbal language to express "love" and other emotions—"has slipped away" from understanding the meaning or absence of meaning in the dog's behavior.

Such personification must play an important role in many owners' interpretations of the plot featuring their relationships with their pets, a plot from which they gain pleasure. To assume that a dog can "thank" (exhibit loyalty and gratitude to a master), one may also consider it necessary to assume that it is able to "think"—to conceptualize loyalty and gratitude in a quasi-human way. But, in this case, what has the owner done for the spayed, moaning dog that deserves thanks? Nothing in the poem provides an answer, unless fealty to a "king" has its own psychological rewards. Shapiro's poem simultaneously bolsters "kind owners'" reassuring narratives and, in exaggerating and multiplying the personifications, as well as using much ambiguity and disjunction, parodies and challenges the premises of the narrative. Whether the dog is in a dense space ("forest") or, later, a sparse one ("desert"), these are tropes of isolation for the relatively powerless dog, and they expose the "cruel" gap between man and his best friend.

In the course of the poem, the master has been represented as "me," then as the dog's "king," as "the addressee," and finally as "you." Thus, according to the poet's narrative displacements, the reader starts out in the position of a mere observer and ends up in that of master, who now possesses the gift of reassurance from the narrator that "the dog thanks [him] in the desert." (Or perhaps this is an implicit rebuke, if we assume that the master has not done his / her best to return the pet's affection but has exiled him to "the desert.") The poem's last two lines may imply a triumph for the owner, but they also trouble the impression of a determinate closure to the poem-story. The repetitive double prepositional phrase, which has appeared often in Shapiro's work, seems to indicate the simple mental "space" of the dog within the bare space of its physical isolation—a double remove from the owner's mental and physical environment—and so the "trace" is the persistent impression or memory that the owner has "left" in / on the dog, whether intentionally or not. However, the line can also signify a more ominous possibility: "you have left" (abandoned) the dog, which is "a trace" of your experience and your potential for kindness, in a far away place. The return of the "trace" in the poem may be comparable to the return of the repressed in psychoanalysis, inducing guilt or a "haunting."

From the beginning to the end of "Winter Work," narrative gestures are present but cannot lead to the kinds of coherence conventionally associated with narrative. The title cannot offer guidance that points in a single direction. The poem itself may be considered a "winter" text, one involving emotional desolation, or "Winter Work" may signify how the poet (who, at least in the beginning, is also the master, even if he cleverly "slips away" from that responsibility) engages in austere questioning of the representation of an animal's mental terrain and its implications for human-animal interaction. The title could refer to the dog's "work" of "prayer" and mourning for the absent master, or to the pet's labor of expressing "thanks" for whatever is thought to be given or withdrawn.

"Winter Work" dramatizes interspecies power relations that may be considered analogous to situations among human beings. For decades, Shapiro has thought, in poetry, about the interaction of poetry and its social contexts and about its value. In his 2002 interview with Joanna Fuhrman, he cites a statement by one of the professors who influenced him most: "'Even your dreams are social,' as Meyer Schapiro suggested, critiquing the surrealists." In his 1990 interview with Joseph Lease, Shapiro speaks of being part of "the generation of '68 that thought they could do something" and approvingly cites the visual artist Irving Petlin's statement, "'I think we held back the full force of the fist of the American empire.'" He identifies "the rage in [his] poetry," discernible "in the photographic cliché of [his] smoking the president of Columbia's cigar)" that originally appeared in *Life* magazine, as "the enormous rage over the immoral war with the Vietnamese," of which he "still continue[s] to think in almost Manichean terms." Shapiro decries "the yielding of the universities . . . , and . . . of the entire society to that war." This interview was conducted near the time that the first Bush administration was contemplating invading Saddam Hussein's Iraq, and so Shapiro probably had current exigencies in mind when he declared: "I regard it as a valuable part of my poetry—the rage against the American empire. I'm still fairly assured that the empire needs to be criticized." However, while he deemed "this anti-imperial theme as a part of" his poetry, he insisted, as though cautioning against narrative continuity: "I don't make it my topic. It's not my burden to be explicitly, dogmatically political."

A Burning Interior has its fair share of poems with something like the "anti-imperial theme." These include "Song for Hannah Arendt" (15), part of the book's long title-sequence, "Christ in Prague" (34), "Pushkin's Prophet" (36–37), "Dream of December Ninth" (68), and "For the Evening Land" (96–97). One especially potent example of how Shapiro uses narrative to think through sociopolitical concerns can be found in "Tall Rock in the Form of an Old Child." The title establishes a relationship between the first and third nouns that will shift several times in the course of the poem. The word "rock" could be taken literally or might be a cliché (placed in a fresh linguistic context) for a person of strong character who, somehow, also has childlike qualities. The poem begins by departing from the concepts in the title and by disabling the literal reading in a complex way:

> A man hid himself
> and lived in a thin rock.
> The king heard his name
> and desired a sick visit.
> But the old man was outside
> and would not come inside.
> The King screamed Old man, weak poet
> visit me—The old child
> replied: You visit me,
> weak king.
>
> (*BI* 28)

The first two lines suggest that the "old child" / man does not embody or seem to embody the rock but is living within the formal structure ("in the form of") of this "thin" (but also "tall"?) rock. But how does one hide "in a rock," as opposed to in a cave? One can't, so

I read the sentence figuratively as a declaration of how the individual dwells "within" the albeit "thin" protection of an attitude—of toughness, psychological solidity—acquired from an external source and still external to the vulnerable "self," which remains hidden.

The rock-dweller is not immune to the summons of the most politically powerful figure in his environment. But does the term "sick visit" imply that the king wishes to cure the "sick" (antisocial?) "hermit" through royal largesse or that the social structure has problems and needs the "old child's" wise counsel? Shapiro keeps both options open, "but the old man" resists the king's gesture by being, paradoxically, "inside" his "rock" and "outside" a sense of his own subjection to the ruler. Angry about this insubordination, the monarch reminds him with the epithet "weak poet" either that he is politically weak or aesthetically inadequate as a poet. Using an echoing reversal, the man posits himself as regal and able to summon. His follow-up statement, "A student / is better than a president," reminds me of the famous picture that Shapiro mentions in the excerpt above from the interview with Lease. Even if this hierarchy-reversing declaration tells us that power corrupts and that eagerness, the Latin root of "student," is morally superior to ambition and social control, it is telling that "president" is substituted for the expected "king." Perhaps this elicits the monarch's "inevitable" agreement (but, ironically, with the idea that a king is preferable to a president): "The king could only agree / and offered him a job. Or cut his neck."

At this point, the narrator's ominous fragment almost "cuts" the "neck" of his burgeoning story. Does the king attempt to co-opt the insolent sap with a promise of gainful employment, or does he execute him for treason and thus show the futility of the "rock's" protection? For now, the "old man" keeps talking back and announces his intention to leave a "place" (near the king) where the "narrator" never exactly situated him:

> The old man said: This jade is a joke, it
> splits and famous rich men
> who take government positions
> lack unity. I am going
> home backwards and hide
> in a secret day: the old way.

(*BI* 28)

The term "jade," signifying not only a precious stone but a worn out horse and a woman of ill repute, makes the king's offer seem relatively worthless because of the linkage with "joke." The arbitrary assumption that "famous rich men" are morally compromised helps the man justify his oppositional stance and his departure; he refuses co-optation.

Next, Shapiro's speaker departs from the story of the king and defiant subject to go back in time to revise the origin of the man's rock dwelling: "He grew up inside a rock / and never strayed from that / thin and watery rock." Perhaps this life-long continuity of place asserts an unchanging unity of attitude that has enabled the man to stand up to the king. But the poet just as suddenly shifts focus from him to "us" in a way that suggests that an individual's will, however rocklike, may be a good example for a community but provides no guarantee that many people can "enter" this "rock" to protect themselves against whatever violently curtails their major freedoms: "Today / the knife mark is on our neck. Holes." Tinged by the violence of this sentence, the concluding five-line strophe pays attention to both the man, "us", and an unspecified "you":

> Thin, because a student's scrawny,
> Wrinkled, like your damaged face.
> Holes, because our clothes are finished.
> (Architecture is drunk like mud.)
> The house of water hides itself.
>   (*BI* 28)

Even if "a student / is better than a President," especially the frighteningly conservative one in the U.S. during whose term Shapiro wrote this poem, the student's "scrawny" frame, as well as the "old child's" time-marred "face," bespeaks vulnerability to political power's severe "mark." Further, poverty's impact is glimpsed in "holes" in "clothes" that are worn out, falling apart. The difficult parenthetical statement hinges on the double meaning of "drunk." Is the psychic "architecture" of the "rock" merely intoxication, which, "like mud," allows no real security? After all, impractical defiance can have disastrous consequences. Or is this "architecture" *imbibed for actual nourishment* by the thirsty self, just as "mud" is absorbed by solid structures?

The final line gives the reader even more trouble than the penultimate one. We had learned in the previous reference to the "rock" that it is not only "thin" but, strangely, "watery," and so it must be the "house of water." But how does the reader coax the figurative potential(s) of this strange concluding personification out of "hiding"? For one thing, the preposition "of" can signify either the house's watery substance or water as "property owner." Perhaps, within the constancy and courage of the human "rock," at one with his "house," there is a fluidity of thinking, a lack of dogmatism that Shapiro has espoused in both his prose and in abstract remarks in poems. In this case, the "water" comprising the philosophical "substance" of the "house" "hides" within its stony fortress to protect itself from the menacing rigidities of the politically powerful.

Note, however, that the assertion that the simultaneously watery, rocky "house . . . hides itself" does not include information about how or why (or from whom) it hides itself. If "child / old man" is unified with his house, then the middle "action" of the poem would suggest that both are hiding from whoever can "cut his neck" and demolish or appropriate the house. If one assumes no unification between dweller and dwelling, the personification is very difficult to explain, because the "house" is a force external to the dweller's will. Further, the final word "itself" emphasizes division of an entity into two: protector and protected. Self-doubling is an answer to vulnerability. This division may point backwards to nouns like "rock," "child," "man," "house," or "water" and retrospectively cause them to be read as locations where differences are collected into a semblance of oneness or, even where oneness "hides" differences.

In modern and contemporary narratives, open-endedness often guides the reader toward two definitive, often opposite choices; Shapiro's narrative poems feature a *multiplicity* of possible references at various stages of a "story's" development that can fragment whatever "rock" would serve as a basis for closure, for final unification (or neat, static bifurcation) of narrative wanderings. Shapiro offers much more narrative material and, at times, the appearance of linear temporal progress than "the taste of a plot" that he has observed in Ashbery. Further, emotional engagement with apparent conflict and complication in the poems is entirely possible, as is an emotional response to the poet's repeated exposure of how departures from stable meaning dwell "dangerously" and meaningfully within unifying possibilities of narrative organization. The will to narrative is powerful and does not surrender to disruption any more than energies of disjunction are snuffed out.

My emphasis on the "uncanny" in Shapiro's narratives should not be confused with a claim that some overarching undecidability (as static, "final" principle) presides over the work and renders it "apolitical." The ideological investments that have appeared in his collections of the last thirty or so years—and the statement in his interview with Lease suggests that this is a subtle but crucial aspect of his ongoing, if discontinuous "narrative"—are just as durable as the poet's concentration on the slipperiness of language and the incompleteness of each available perspective. In his interview with Lease, Shapiro links narrative with politics, family, and "decentered" movement:

> The narrative, which implies the family that has a beginning, middle, and end (children or mothers dying) and the public situation (which is framed most darkly by the Holocaust and the meaning of political oppression in our century up to and including things that are still taking place in the Middle East—the transition from victim to victor and back again in nation-states): those are the dark nomadic edges of my poetry.

In "Tall Rock in the Form of an Old Child," is there any doubt that the poet's solidarity remains with the blurry figure of the young / old child / student / man in his difficult struggle with authority, or that the king is subject to skepticism until he is removed from the narrative? Nevertheless, words' multiplicity complicates "characters'" identity, their impact on other figures, and their internalization of others' influences. It is conceivable that a reader's emotional involvement in the "fates" of these "people" could come into play, but in the long run, this is less prominent than the attention Shapiro's structurings, departures, and re-structurings bring to fluctuations of social and aesthetic dynamics.

NOTES

1. David Shapiro, *John Ashbery: An Introduction to the Poetry* (New York: Columbia University Press, 1979), 61. Shapiro has not written about Ashbery since 1979. Although Ashbery has published a great deal since then, his work has not

moved in an appreciably more narrative direction, and so there is no reason to think that Shapiro has revised his assessment.

2. Ibid., 4–7.

3. For evidence of my claims about Shapiro's influences and affiliations, see three interviews in particular: Joseph Lease, "After the New York School: Interview with David Shapiro," *Pataphysics Magazine* (1990) http://www.pataphysicsmagazine.com/shapiro_interview.html (Accessed 9/5/05); Joanna Fuhrman, "Pluralist Music: An Interview with David Shapiro," *Rain Taxi Online* (Fall 2002) http://www.raintaxi.com/online/2002fall/shapiro.shtml ; and Elizabeth Bassford, "The Beautiful View: Lunch with David Shapiro," *Exoterica* (2003) http://www.exoterica.org/shapirointerview.html . In these interviews, Shapiro often underlines the interpenetration of various aesthetic modes; for example, in the Fuhrman interview, he recalls how, when Kenneth Koch showed him Ashbery's poetry collected in *The Tennis Court Oath*, he only "fell in love with it" after finding that "it reminded [him] of a Rauschenberg collage." Further reference to the Fuhrman interview is sufficiently located in the text.

4. Bob Perelman, "for *Change*," *In the American Tree*. Ed. Ron Silliman. (Orono, ME: National Poetry Foundation, 1986), 489.

5. Ibid., 490.

6. Robert Gluck, "Long Note on New Narrative," *Narrativity* 1, nd. *http://www.sfsu.edu/~newlit/narrativity/issue_one/gluck.html.*

7. Ibid. This kind of hybridity, of course, is important to experimental poets who may not fit the subject positions that Gluck mentions but are at odds with mainstream culture's representation of them for other reasons. See, for example, the analysis of Chinese-American poet John Yau's advocacy of hybridity in my *"A Different Sense of Power": Problems of Community in Late-Twentieth Century U.S. Poetry* (Rutherford, NJ: Fairleigh Dickinson University Press, 2001), 57–73.

8. Ibid. I assume that Gluck's mention of "total continuity" and "total disjunction" is intended to represent affective states, since neither extreme seems possible in practical terms for a writer or reader.

In an interview with Gary Sullivan, *Read Me* 4 (Spring/Summer 2001), http://home.jps.net/~nada/killian.html, Kevin Killian, a major figure in the "New Narrative," acknowledges that his group was "reacting against the Language Poets and what [they] took to be their program of abolishing narrative, the lack of fun in their writing," despite agreement "with everything they were doing except the density of their non-fun," but he also notes that the "New Narrativists" "were shocked . . . to find that" the Language "poets were the first ones to soften up towards [them] and invite them into [their] world."

9. Mark Wallace, "Definitions in Process/Definitions as Process/Uneasy Collaborations: Language and Postlanguage Poetries," *Flashpoint*. Web Issue 2 (Spring 1998) *http://www.flashpointmag.com/postlang.html.*

10. Ibid. Arguably, various innovative poets who are older than most "postlanguage poets" but are not affiliated with Language Poetry might also be said to serve the functions that Wallace is describing. I have already mentioned John Yau; other poets include Mei-mei Berssenbrugge, Joseph Donahue, Andrew Joron, Ann Lauterbach, Eileen Tabios, and my coeditor Joseph Lease and another con-

tributor to the volume, Stephen Paul Miller. During their formative years as poets, Donahue, Lease, and Miller absorbed Shapiro's influence.

11. Joseph Lease, "After the New York School: David Shapiro Interview." Further reference to the interview is sufficiently located in the text.

12. Mark Wallace, Bernstein and Perelman's inclusion of poetic strategies that Wallace views as "postlanguage" may reflect a dialogue with younger poets, including the former writers' own graduate students, but it may have as much or more to do with the poets' renegotiation in the eighties and nineties of their long-standing engagement with Objectivism, Black Mountain, the San Francisco Renaissance, the New York School, and experimental writers of color like Nathaniel Mackey and Kamau Brathwaite. This kind of analysis is a major feature of Ron Silliman's popular blog, from which his chapter in this book is taken.

For the ways in which *Talisman*, among other journals, is transforming the understanding of contemporary poetry history, see the diverse essays on Language Poetry, the New York School, "Neo-Surrealism," "visionary" experimentation, post-Black Mountain, feminist, African-American and Asian-American innovation, what Wallace would call "postlanguage" poets, and poetry influenced by more than one "school" in *The World in Time and Space: Towards a History of Innovative American Poetry in Our Time*. Ed. Edward Foster and Joseph Donahue (Jersey City, NJ: Talisman House, 2002). This volume constitutes issues 23 to 26 of the journal.

In *The Poetry of David Shapiro* (Rutherford, NJ: Fairleigh Dickinson University Press, 1993), although I discuss concepts of representation a great deal, especially in the second chapter, "Desire, Representation, and Critique," I do not foreground Shapiro's use of narrative strategies. However, the book includes close readings of such poems as "To an Idea" (1983) and "After a Lost Original," the first section of a sequence of that name, and "You Are Tall and Thin," another poem in the sequence, that possess discernible narrative elements. This article is an acknowledgment of my prior omission, and a corrective gesture.

Distorted Figures: Mannerist Similes and the Body in David Shapiro's Poetry

Tim Peterson

AT THE BEGINNING OF A LONG SEQUENCE IN DAVID SHAPIRO'S BOOK *After A Lost Original*, we encounter the following passage:

> There is the gate or the copy of a gate
> Blood outlines the gate, like a nude
> A pink flower like a tree emits sparks
> They gather into a yellow blue fragmentary flower
> In the other space, formed by flowers torn apart
> It bites the ground, like a blackened moon.
>
> (25)

Only six lines into a postmodern poet's book, and we have already been confronted with three similes. Not only is the number remarkable; perhaps stranger is the fact that they are *similes* (rather than metaphors)—an archaic device few contemporary poets in the avant-garde have dared employ since Pound's development of imagism.

Indeed, the classic definition of simile is: a more overt form of metaphor which compares two things using the words "like" or "as." Most poets since modernism, if they employ metaphors at all, have done so using direct presentation of imagery rather than making the effort to include the "like" or "as" word that shows a speaker is doing the comparing. Similes function much like metaphors, the classic definition of which was developed by the literary critic I. A. Richards in *The Philosophy of Rhetoric*. Richards said that a metaphor consists of two terms: the tenor (the thing literally being talked about) and the vehicle (the thing it is being compared to). Tenor and vehicle in this definition share a "ground," a similarity which this comparison brings out.[1] In the commonly used example "Achilles is a lion in battle," the tenor would be Achilles and the vehicle would be the lion. The ground which connects the two would be the comparative ferocity with which they conduct themselves in battle. Note that this usage is preferable to a clumsy ordinary locution such as "Achilles was pretty intense and aggressive in the battle today" which does not seem to achieve the same impact as the previous metaphorical phrase. Metaphors lend language a vividness and intensity and allow us to express things that literal description cannot.

However, if we look closely at similes in the Shapiro excerpt just quoted, something strange begins to occur. What does the fact that "blood outlines the gate" (presumably the tenor) have in common with "a nude" (presumably the vehicle)? Furthermore, what does "a pink flower" have in common with a tree that "emits sparks," or a personified flower that "bites the ground" have in common with "a blackened moon"? These similes do not appear to share a "ground" which connects tenor and vehicle in the usual way. They may in some way have private meaning for the poet, or one may try to intuit a kind of surreal similarity by using a great deal of extrapolation, but by all *accounts* to a reader, as comparisons they are truly "groundless." "The earth is under us / Like cheap non-fading wallpaper" (L).

What are we to make of these seemingly excessive and superfluous gestures, in which their areas of unlikeness seem to be larger than any potential area of likeness (if indeed the latter does exist). One way to look at them is as examples of mannerism. Shapiro developed an interest in John Ashbery's use of this strategy (as derived from Roussel) in his early study *John Ashbery: An Introduction to the Poetry*:[2]

> Later Ashbery wittily employed another device of Roussel: the specious simile, "the kind that tells you less than you would know if the thing were stated flatly" (interview). In lieu of the organic and necessary simile, Ashbery learned from the French master an extravagance of connection that leads one nowhere, as in "as useless as a ski in a barge," though this example is perhaps still too suggestive. "As useless as a ski" would be Ashbery's paradigmatic revision (interview).

Shapiro in this book emphasizes the fact that these types of devices act as "mannerist" elements in Ashbery's poetry, and the comparison helps illuminate what is so successful about their excessiveness: "In its bizarre suavity, its unrealities, its sudden discontinuities, its constant theatricality, its inordinate fondness for framing devices, Mannerism no longer seems to be anything but our central precursor."[3]

There are certainly many similes in Shapiro's poetry which can be interpreted (and illuminated) using this framework. For example, the instances of this figure in Shapiro's early poetry, beginning with *The Page-Turner*, often display a proliferation of unnecessary or digressive information: "The pulses we receive remain suspicious / Like the hazardous decisions of a night after which we will / see quite differently" (13). The royal "we" of the speaker here, in describing a heart tremor, attempts to expand his initial observation by comparing it to a bizarrely elaborate situation, "the hazardous decisions of a night after which we will see quite differently," which digressively obfuscates the meaning of what he might be talking about, in a fashion not unlike John Ashbery's poetry. Rather than providing a comparison to something unlike the thing being talked about and thereby focusing meaning through a comparison of like and unlike qualities, here we are simply led into further abstractions.

Reading similar tropes in Shapiro's recent poetry this way would not be inaccurate, either: "Perhaps this voice never existed like a lake / Perhaps this translation never existed like a gift my child draws" (*BI* 68). These two digressive and confounding gestures make comparisons in which the terms, as before, do not seem to have any ground in common. One could conceivably repeat such gestures over and over, if this was their only consequence. Ashbery's simile "as useless as a ski" is so effective as a parody particularly because it displays the potentially folksy air of having been recycled from some vague American idiom, and this double-codes and thus defuses any potential pathos. Reproducibility of gesture is also an important resource for Shapiro, who has pursued his own romantically antiromantic investigation of "the copy," but without Ashbery's emphasis on degraded language: "One might call it tracing a hyacinth, or traces of a hyacinth. / Like traces on a blackboard. / Or tracing the window from a neoclassicism upon a blackboard" (TI 37). While this passage from Shapiro's poem "Venetian Blinds" appears to be an example of another superfluous simile, it already starts to resist this definition. The hyacinth and the blackboard both feel as if they are somehow real objects, with consequences. There is less humor or elaborate kidding around; there seems to be on the contrary a serious insistence in these anaphoric repetitions.

As the movement of excess in art which appeared at the end of the Renaissance and charted the deterioration of neoclassical systems of perspective, mannerism can be a useful lens for examining Shapiro's own "belated" poetry. However, the Ashberyian take on this doesn't completely explain Shapiro's inordinate fondness for the simile in particular. One might ask, what do similes allow Shapiro to do that is unique to his own work? One answer might be that we need to look outside Ashbery's notion of the "specious simile" and possibly outside the understanding of Mannerism itself as a mostly decorative or ornamental movement. The mannerist similes that Shapiro employs in his poems are constitutive as well as decorative, functional as well as digressive. They signify not only through the pathos and humor with which they fail to fulfill the functional contract we expect of them, but also through a larger allegory about the body which persists throughout this poet's work.

In Shapiro's poetry, framing devices such as similes have consequences for the world of words they depict. Shapiro's poems create neither a linear narrative nor an original "scene" through a window but instead propose a preposterous exfoliation of poetic machinery which creates multiple points of interest. In "Rivulet near the Truth," the speaker begins with a declaration about "sunken rocks," but then launches into a series of similes which derail the establishment of a consistent scene or context:

> Sunken rocks are sunless
> Like a fence in iniquity
> Or a hedge in oblivion
> Or sunshine at supper
> Like the Supreme Being in surgery
> Restrained by oscillating powers
> Sweeping the dirty body
> Useless as if agreeable stuff
> Like saccharine might look upon
> Love's clean teeth.
>
> (*L*)

The first three comparisons here make a kind of sense: they are talking about a row of partially-submerged objects (the "rivulet" of the title) and thus nodding to a theme of secrecy. As we progress further through these images however, the comparisons make less sense. One has to do a lot of work to attempt to figure out what "sunken rocks are sunless" might have in common with "sunshine at supper." The two things do not seem alike except perhaps as an ironic opposition, or an elaborate hidden connection. And how are sunken rocks like "the Supreme Being in surgery / Restrained by oscillating power"? The potentially cosmological answer would appear to be partially submerged like the rocks themselves. By the time a reader reaches the latter image, having already passed through four comparisons, she might inquire: which is the real thing and which is the imaginary thing it's being compared to? Why all the framing and reframing in this poem? Shapiro's speaker expounds on these problems further:

> There are two kinds of sleep
> Orthodox and paradoxical
> During orthodox there are no dreams
> But normal diplomatic relations
> Like a sentence made up to include
> The sleepers of the whole alphabet.
>
> (*L*)

Apparently waking, the world in which "normal diplomatic relations" might occur, is not an option, or has been collapsed into or confused with merely another kind of sleep. Indeed, in a world where similes and framing take center stage, the question of what is the original and what is the copy, what is sleeping and what is waking, becomes confused.

So these odd comparisons do affect and help structure the "world" of the poem: closer examination reveals them to be load-bearing structures. In contrast to the sense of ornament implied in Ashbery's theory of the "specious simile," Arnold Hauser points out that mannerism's turn away from a cohesive perspectival system creates a crisis of depiction in which the hierarchies of this space are disrupted: "Mannerism begins by breaking up the Renaissance structure of space and the scene to be represented into separate, not merely externally separate but also inwardly differently organized, parts. . . . Motifs which seem to be of only secondary significance for the real subject of the picture are often overbearingly prominent, whereas what is apparently the leading theme is devalued and suppressed."[4] The type of phenomenon that Hauser describes finds its manifestation in Shapiro's poetry through both distortions of space and distortions of the body. One of the more dramatic symptoms of this sectioning-off of "realist" or "naturalist" space is the way in which Shapiro's speaker yokes together two disparate scenes through the use of a strategy I will refer to as "spatial metonymy." Such a use of the simile occurs in "An Exercise in Futility," in which the poet-speaker addresses a mentor:

> You whom I had loved for years like a monumental door leading to
> An exterior interior: to get to this door you climbed a tiny, tinny
>   podium
> And there two mirrors poured into each other
> In a maroon room covered up with dust of bricks and books.
>   (*TI* 17)

The stiff and elaborate architectural diction here of "a monumental door leading to / an exterior interior" throws into stark relief the dramatic unlikeness between this scene and the potentially sentimental reminiscence, "you whom I had loved for years," in the process diffusing any recognizable or naturalistic pathos. The indefiniteness of syntax and the use of the imperfect tense make the comparison even stranger: what is being compared to the monumental door, "you," the action of having loved for years, or "I"? Unable to clearly parse this simile, a reader encounters it primarily as a segue device that connects two scenes and that renders both of them as a consequence equally real and dreamlike.

The scene of the monumental door, which in the terms of official metaphorical parlance would be the vehicle (the imagined thing that the tenor is compared to), here has become the reality of the rest of the poem, which takes place in the "room covered up with the dust of bricks and books." Yet this is not just a situation in which the vehicle has been introduced before the tenor and a reversal has occurred, because the entire piece hinges around the relationship between this "I" and this "you," who are both very real. There's an additionally confounding blurring that occurs between you and I as a result of the simile, like the two mirrors pouring into each other. The common theme among these images seems to be a strange warping of space initiated by the door which leads to the paradoxical "exterior interior."

Such distortions are examples of the types of condensation and displacement that Freud says we find in dreams. Thomas Fink describes this spatial effect as "deterritorialization" via Deleuze and Guattari.[5] Another way to think of this juxtaposition is as "spatial metonymy," ways in which the poet might place two objects next to one another in order to figure a deeper relationship between them.[6] There is something like this latter notion in Jacques Lacan's discussion of metonymy as the functional term in a metaphor: "The creative spark of the metaphor does not spring from the presentation of two images, that is, of two signifiers equally actualized. It flashes between two signifiers one of which has taken the place of the other in the signifying chain, the occulted signifier remaining present through its (metonymic) connexion with the rest of the chain."[7] In this scheme what enlivens a figure is the "spark" that derives from spatial juxtaposition between one object and another, inviting a comparison in order to expose the "occulted" signifier or similarity between the two parts. However, in a great deal of Shapiro's poetry, the partially-submerged nature of his figures and his extended personal allegories guarantee that a reader often comes away with the effect of a figure whose ground (or occulted signifier) has been effectively hidden from sight. Since the terms of his similes share no ground in the usual sense, this "spark" of sublimated metonymy as repressed term or Id has been dispersed throughout the whole figure, and thus the territory of the subconscious is strangely superimposed over that of the real: it's everywhere and nowhere. The resulting dramatic divergence creates a lively sense of dreamlike non sequitur:

> Now only adverbs
> mounting into a series with a sigh
> carried along then like India-ink bottles
> punctured by the subway into prayer.
> (*PT* 44)

> You are high and delegate authority
> Like a lake.
> The night dies like a ninny on the wall.
> (*ALO* 16)

In these situations, the emphasis for a reader is cast back onto the manipulation of the poem-dream's space via a principle of nextness, as the operative function of the speaker's desire. Although the nature of this desire in individual gestures remains mysterious, there is nevertheless an effort here to create a momentarily sincere emotion by rendering the usual pathos of such attempts at simile temporarily unrecognizable, or what Freud calls "*unheimlich.*" Sometimes the juxtaposition evokes a kind of odd tenderness through the very strangeness and intimacy of its non sequitur:

> Lightly you touch me
> Paper on which I write
> Problems have turned into snow at night
> Like a little car abandoned in the midst of vague terror.
>
> (*L*)

In "Stay Stay Stay Stay" Shapiro quotes a tender metaphor from Eluard (the personal significance of which is never quite explained) but which enacts this metonymic principle of desire: "You are standing on my eyelids / And your hair is in my hair" (*L*). The placement of bodies next to one another has consequences for the ordering of the poem-world through the medium of the speaker's voice which figures possibilities of both intimacy and pluralism in strange new ways.

But exterior space is not the only thing affected by this breakdown. Indeed, Hauser's sense of the dissolution of classical perspective also finds its manifestation for Shapiro in the symptom of distorted bodies, the body "turning and twisting, bending and writhing under the pressure of the mind."[8] This passage from "The Counter-Example" finds the speaker-painter struggling with this very issue, in reference to his own efforts to imitate nature:

> You did not want to paint twisting life in red points
> But randomly following the paper, you twisted the lines
>
> Distorted as a man following a dolphin
> Struggling not to surface but diving to drown
>
> In a drifting wet imperturbability.
>
> (*TI* 23)

Shapiro's abrupt transition here from a scene of painting on paper to a distorted figure following a dolphin is confounding in the richest ways. These statements yoke together two apparently unrelated scenes using a simile in combination with the tonal words "twisted" and "distorted." The image is encrusted with multiple metaphors:

how is a man following a dolphin distorted, unless it is by the water which obscures his form as he dives into the depths, just as the specific content underlying this metaphor seems somehow submerged, just out of reach? Yet at other moments Shapiro's distorted bodies take on the quality of something more akin to Freud's polymorphously perverse, as in the following passages from "The Devil's Trill Sonata":

> There we are, like two crystals joined together
> In a specific rational manner, twin city in full night
> With set arias and binoculars adapted for use at the opera,
> And you so silky stretched over and under me like a steel frame....
>
> Ophelia is some sort of fluid
> The silk cloth is rubbed and she flows
> Her comparatively small body wades into the stream
> She has been rubbed off and migrates into the silk
>
> You made a rough sketch of the swordplay
> And the sword tilts
> Hamlet drifts like water through the pipes
> The earth is a magnet that can be switched on and off,
>   But where is that switch?
>
> (*L*)

Here the distortion of bodies creates an effect not unlike the previously described uses of spatial metonymy. When bodies no longer obey the usual physical laws, they become oddly spatialized and take on characteristics not unlike those of landscape or architecture. The "stuff" of bodies and the "stuff" of nature become oddly intertwined.

This sense of the body as simultaneously inside, outside, and all around one owes something to its strange quality of concretion via the medium of the speaker's voice, as a "wandering part of the body" (*HBA* 56). I derive this concept from Tenney Nathanson's influential study *Whitman's Presence*. In this book Nathanson evokes a strange, labile space in which the poet's voice acts as an "eternal float of solution" through its manipulation of various objects: "Associated with the insides such exteriors sequester, this animating force is typically figured in Whitman's work as a flood that creates all individual forms from out of its ceaseless flowing ... it results in the momentary dissolution of blocking surfaces and the ecstatic mingling of no-longer bounded forms."⁹ Employing Derrida's discussion of Husserl's phenomenal voice as "interiorized," Nathanson develops a trope of a ghostly body which owes something to this sense of interiority by means of its various manifestations in the trope of voice. But since Shapiro is a different kind of poet than Whitman, what I am talking about has less to do with the poet's voice as ghostly manifestation to a present reader (figured through writing) than with the notion of an ambivalent relationship toward one's own body and toward nature, the sense of not feeling quite at home in one's body. Unlike Whitman, whose voice is synonymous with the creation of his presence in relation to a reader, there is a belated sense in Shapiro's poetry that his voice has somehow always been present, and the poet is instead using the trope in his word-magic manipulations primarily as a means of exploring now dreamlike, now real scenarios.

Therefore I would like to propose a slightly different notion of interiority which is sometimes at odds with (but nevertheless sees itself in relation to) the physical body. Paul Schilder in his book *The Image and Appearance of the Body* proposes a "postural model of the body" which parallels the physical body but which nevertheless has its own autonomy:¹⁰

> It is to the existence of these "schemata" that we owe the power of projecting our recognition of posture, movement, and locality beyond the limits of our own bodies. . . . Anything which participates in the conscious movement of our bodies is added to the model of ourselves and becomes part of these schemata: a woman's power of localization may extend to the feather in her hat.
>
> When a leg has been amputated, a phantom appears; the individual still feels his leg and has a vivid impression that it is still there. He may also forget about his loss and fall down. This phantom, this animated image of the leg, is the expression of the body schema.

The impressions of interiority thus sometimes diverge from the external world, and an accurate mimesis of nature as such is neither particularly possible nor desirable, a fact of which Shapiro reminds us: "The lion's mane has successive rows of flames / In your missing hand you would have held the lion" (*L*).

This oblique and often conflicted relationship between interior and exterior body finds vivid articulation in Shapiro's poem "An Afternoon with a Lion":

> Hand over hand you were getting into the lion,
> Sniffing palm trees and floating upon the lion
> Towards the lion and up to the lion.
>
> In the seventh frame you slipped above the lion
> Into the white sky beyond each lion,
> Around the lion and with the lion.
>
> Now under the lion, smiling under the lion
> It's a light green day edges toward the lion,
> Towards the lion and up to the lion.
>
> But how is one to get out of the lion,
> One's hat and stick sticking out of the lion,
> Around the lion and with the lion?
>
> (*L*)

Here the lion, like one of Shapiro's famous polysemous puns, stands for multiple things. As an actual creature, it is not very convincing, because one cannot occupy the same space as a lion without being eaten. Instead the speaker here has a strange polymorphously embodied relationship to this creature: he is now inside it, now above it or next to it, but he cannot get away from it — he is somehow attached. The lion here acts as a stand-in for both the physical body and for nature itself, and the speaker enacts in a humorously surreal way the relationship of interiority to this external body, which seems as foreign as a wild animal. It is worth noting that the speaker's attempt to flee the lion in the last stanza ("days away from the lion") is ultimately foiled by nothing less than the poetic form itself, the "traditions" of literature in which the poet works: the closing couplet of the villanelle demands a continued and perhaps eternal engagement with this "lion."

It is likewise not coincidental that similes, another such belated constraint of literary form, appear so frequently in Shapiro's poetry. Shapiro's mannerist similes, his "distorted figures," are precisely the site at which distortions of nature and of the body intersect. Mediating between interior and exterior through the multiplication of framing devices, they continually negotiate this boundary which has been rendered anxiously amorphous by the dissolution of classical perspective. We are confronted with such a passage near the end of "Rivulet Near the Truth:"

> The vista out this window makes
> a plea in a vague style
> pale as a Persian blind
> giggling like refined gold
> tempted to please like a pill: Look
> The loophole is opening now
> looming like a looking glass
> the thirsty soul examines
> itself and we each other
> As it is said you hug
> A belief as the playhouse is hidden.
>
> (*L*)

Veering away from the exterior into a process of narrating interior perception itself, this passage depicts a frustrated version of a vista. Thomas Fink in his book *The Poetry of David Shapiro* points out that Shapiro's work continually looks for an outside "truth" of some kind but continually bumps up against the mediations of the self in language.[11] I would agree with this assessment, but would substitute the term "nature" for "truth" in my analysis of Shapiro's staged attempts at mimesis. This passage from "House (Blown Apart)" engages in a similar attempt: "I can see the traces of old work / Embedded in this page like your bed / Within a bed. My old desire to live!" (*HBA* 15). Here the traces of interiority in the form of memories or dreams ("old work") mingle with a background which has also been strangely interiorized: the page / bed. Not only does this scenario propose a paradoxical space in which waking both is and is not an option, but it proposes a strange mixing of interior and exterior experience.

These and other excerpts illustrate a continuing allegory throughout Shapiro's poetry of the body as exploded ("blown apart") and strewn across or mingled with the landscape beyond it. The word "like" in Shapiro's similes constitutes what remains of that body's boundary, both in terms of phenomenology and in terms of their own belated relation to literary tradition. As a wandering part of the body, voice represents the presence of a speaker, and here the word "like" similarly figures the presence of that speaker actively making comparisons and motivated in this enterprise by desire.

> The very expression "figure of speech" implies that in metaphor, as in the other tropes or turns, discourse assumes the nature of a body by displaying forms and traits which usually characterize the human

face, man's "figure"; it is as though the tropes have to discourse a quasi-bodily externalization. By providing a kind of figurability to the message, the tropes make discourse appear.[12]

Ricoeur's view of metaphor as "quasi-bodily externalization" dramatizes the way in which Shapiro's similes act as extensions of interiority. In the interior body's perception of external nature, one can go up to that boundary, but it becomes unclear whether one actually reaches an unmediated experience. In fact, this is the real definition of mannerism as a constitutive crisis for representation: it is the imitation of culture rather than nature.

> But the artistic solution is always a derivative, a structure dependent in the final analysis on classicism, and originating in a cultural, not a natural experience, whether it is expressed in the form of a protest against classical art or seeks to preserve the formal achievements of this art. We are dealing here, in other words, with a completely self-conscious style, which bases its forms not so much on the particular object as on the art of the preceding epoch.[13]

While Shapiro would no doubt fall under the "protest against" part of Hauser's definition, there are, nonetheless, remnants of classicism in his poetry, in his actual subject matter (Socrates, the Erecthion, etc.), in his use of inherited forms such as villanelles and iambic meter, and in "naked devices" used for framing likeness such as the simile. But it has all been radically altered and distorted by the (post)modern experience of interiority. This belated yet nonetheless revolutionary cultural work performs a "thinking through" in its dramatic and lively mimesis of attempting to extend outward.

Notes

1. I. A. Richards, *The Philosophy of Rhetoric*, 1939 (New York: Oxford University Press, 1965), 90–97.

2. David Shapiro, *John Ashbery: An Introduction to the Poetry* (New York: Columbia University Press, 1979), 17.

3. Ibid., 5.

4. Arnold Hauser, *The Social History of Art* (New York: Routledge, 2003), 93.

5. Thomas Fink, The *Poetry of David Shapiro* (Rutherford, NJ: Fairleigh Dickinson University Press, 1993), 89.

6. Lecture notes, Tenney Nathanson, course on Modernist Poetry, University of Arizona, Tucson, 2002.

7. Jacques Lacan, *Ecrits* (New York: Norton, 1977), 157.

8. Arnold Hauser, *The Social History of Art*, 96.

9. Tenney Nathanson, *Whitman's Presence: Body, Voice, and Writing in Leaves of Grass* (New York: New York University Press, 1992), 59.

10. Paul Schilder, *The Image and Appearance of the Human Body* (New York: International Universities Press, 1978), 13.

11. Thomas Fink, *The Poetry of David Shapiro*, 56.

12. Paul Ricoeur, "The Metaphorical Process," in *On Metaphor*, ed. Sheldon Sacks (Chicago: University of Chicago Press, 1979), 142.

13. Arnold Hauser, *The Social History of Art*, 91.

For Dust Thou Art
—for David Shapiro

Timothy Liu

I

The field was finally sown.
The evening fallen.
Perhaps some sweetness in the air.
So he began to read.
His woman in the other room.
Adjacent to his solitude.
Neither in despair nor free to roam.
Caught as yet in the about-to-be.
It would take some time.
The book he held approximating field.
Of course the consequences.
Unseen mouths to feed.
As seasons changed from room to room.
Winter here. Spring over there.
It would take some time.
The woman he held.
Their emptiness already in full bloom.

II

Had you been so adept through a series of polished hoops?
All of your training amounting to this.
Countless titles and certificates affixed to a wall.
That sort of thing.
Halos you couldn't pass through now.
Some said you were the doctor but were you patient?
This was the start of many confusions.

Working out salvation by the sweat of your furrowed brow.
The shape of your body afflicted with what it was.
What you were becoming all along.
Could regimens really keep the future at bay?
Suffering, death, etc.
All of the usual calamities that kept you employed.
Congress with whomever sought your care.
Now left benighted on pastures where you had once put out.

III

Who told thee thou wast naked? the story goes.
We had to begin somewhere.
Even in disbelief.
As the veil was rent in infant sleep never having known it.
I can feel it in my bones but I cannot see it.
A mother refusing to give suck.
If not this day if not her voice then even so.
Inhalation. Exhalation.
Was the body only messenger to the message?
This milk will cost you.
You ask the world for bread but are given stone.
Systole. Diastole. A Sisyphian stone.
With all the dead around you now coming into view.
Each with a stone not of their choosing.
Nor of their making.
The eternal journey from heart to mind less than three-feet long.
I relax my shoulders, my shoulders are relaxed.
I relax my liver, my liver is relaxed.
And so on.
With our tailbones anchored to the center of the earth.

House Blown Apart

Jeremy Gilbert-Rolfe

THE TWENTIETH CENTURY IS TOO PREOCCUPIED WITH THE POETIC dimension of everyday life to be able to spare much attention for poetry itself. Advertising and politics—more or less the same thing—provide a discourse so entirely detached from the world, while completely obscuring it, as to keep the general public's imagination locked into a poesis of the banal, a poesis in which symbolic instructions lead unerringly into another entirely symbolic formulation, in which desire is paraded and resolved without ever coming down to earth (wear this and you'll feel great despite the fact that you have, in fact, absolutely no economic future), in which phobias are aired out at no risk (bomb Tripoli and Benghazi and you will feel imperial and will have demonstrated power). It was always like this but conceivably not always so extremely *linguified*, so liquefied by the domination of language, of a world in which there are in the beginning so many names that one never gets to the thing—in the beginning were words, and as a consequence the world has been indefinitely deferred.

Viewed from outside—I am not a poet—poets seem, generally speaking, to have responded to this condition by preserving, in flagrant contradiction to all that categorizes the twentieth century, the idea of the private. Specifically private experience, an elaborate concept in an age where it has been demonstrated that a vast majority of young people can only read when music is being played in the background, in other words, when their bodies are not entirely focused on the text. Or, to put it more precisely, when the text is not exclusively a written one, but is instead a writing supplemented by a connection to the outside which has no relationship to it—and which unwrites it, therefore, even as it is being read, by eroding it, taking the reader away from it, distancing her or him from it, accompaniment by subversion. (For we understand that the old fantasy, that this bit of Beethoven *matches*, because it shares, in some assumed but nonetheless demonstrable way, the same classicist principles that underlie the text by, say, Mallarmé that I read while I play Ludwig on the gramophone, is definitely out the window: this bit of Shapiro conceivably has something in common with, but quite a lot that separates it from, absolutely anything I might put on the stereo while I read, including Beethoven.)

I have introduced Shapiro parenthetically, and it is thus that poets get into the latter part of our century as interstitial figures who attract our attention, when they do, through the strength of their irrelevance. Once, in the dreary slaveholding societies which were the classical world, as well as in the filthy and loud-mouthed village-bound societies of the Celts and the Goths, poets were central to the social order. Now, in the world of total passive-aggression provided by late capitalism (of power which remains unchanging through constant simulation of access to itself, triumph of the slave owner, triumph of the soft-spoken), they are peripheral to it in all respects but one. But they remain, as ever, the only people who know how the language actually works. And like all people who are privy to special knowledge, they accordingly pretend that they are chiefly concerned with just keeping it alive. Like all custodians, they are instead, *pace* Foucault, changing it by the minute, and are themselves quite unable to keep up with the change.

One is tempted to accuse poets of flight, of not standing up for themselves. The history of modern poetry seems in general to be one of a veritable rush to the fringe, the margin, to, I suppose, the *Wasteland*. But the example of those who remained at the center suggests otherwise, giving strength to the defense that their condition was in fact thrust upon them. In England, where the nonpublic is not really supposed to take place at all in any way that could be articulated ("He never asked personal questions, he was an English gentleman, and as such not very interested in persons") poetry has long since been something which was done by people from Wales or Ireland, where the conditions of the late Bronze Age still prevail. English poetry has sacrificed—sort of immolated—itself on the altar of the social. The mere mention of an English last name in connection with poetry causes fear and the expectation of an arid little—sometimes not even little—piece on steam engines, the decline of something having to do with learning or feeling, or, a related subject and theme, injustice of a psycho-social-sexual sort. So one should not suppose that a poet such as Shapiro is where he is, in relation to the voice and power of the television, through any fault of his own. There isn't anywhere else to go.

> Or was it from here
> You might have mutilated the questions
> From the point of view of every right of dissolution
> What the day knew or straight back to the cat's brain
> Laughing beside homemade pillows
> Homemade theodicy
> But what one doesn't know are the geometries
> that might have described or created
> that possible world
> "House (IV)" (*HBA* 84)

There seem to be three, or three and a half, historical sources for the possible world described or created by Shapiro's poetry—three and a half historicomythical worlds. There is, to put the half first, American poetry since the Second World War. The New York poets with whom he has long had, as a New York poet, a variety of connections and associations—Frank O'Hara being the first to publish his work, Ashbery the subject of his PhD dissertation. Behind that, or along with it, is a more scholarly view of mainstream modernism—Pound, Eliot, Stevens, Cummings, in a word, *them*—than one finds, for the most part, in the New York poets of the preceding generation. Then there is French symbolism, from which Shapiro seems to derive quite a lot in the way of lexical organization (poetic order) itself and, through that, of images which reunite the abstract with the body:

> And I stood up alone like a girl in the street
> alone in father's shop, where I
> mistook time for a hat.
> "Another Marschallin" (*HBA* 45)

and also:

> The door a diamond externally but taken internally almost a wall
> Where there is no door, notched men seeking the edges
> For our part to slide through as it will be present again
> our breasts stained by paper.
> "A Book of Doors" (*HBA* 66)

Shapiro's use of French symbolism is different from that of other Americans in the extremism of its playfulness. This is probably what annoys people most about his poetry. It tends to engage in pathos without being earnest:

> School? Painting? Oh we are taking a bus
> Death says it's ridiculous to give you more time to polish
> "Taking a Ferry" (*HBA* 23)

Like other American poets, Shapiro uses symbolism to produce images and scenes of childhood on the one hand and of unspoken desire on the other. In Shapiro's lexicon the point of view of the child is distant and subject to scenes of dissolution:

> Mother is burning her father
> In layers of newspaper.
> "A Visit from the Past" (*HBA* 21)

or of impossible archetype:

> My father the soldier stands upon the rock
> "A Study of Two Late July Fourths" (*HBA* 46)

or of images which make sense only as components of recall, of a search for origins:

> In memory while the profile of liberty rusts, in memory of the green
> Journals like a child at the center of the earth
> "In Memory of Poetry" (*HBA* 29)

For me—unfamiliar with the byways while knowing the highway, ignorant of the bylaws while generally familiar with the law—the force deployed by Shapiro is symbolist and weirdly revisionist in its attitude to symbolism, and American in a very anti-American way, wanting to use American materials and American roughness and flippancy and frivolity and (of course) intimacy, but insisting on a *collaging* which belongs to modernism rather than to folk art.

The weirdness of Shapiro's use of symbolism lies in its willed regressiveness. Symbolism was *the* pre-Freudian moment, in which all that psychoanalysis would ever say, and, perhaps, far more than it would ever see, was spelled out by poets. But it *was* pre-Freudian.

Shapiro returns to the workshop of Mallarmé and Verlaine, the place of the moment's pretense to significance and the book's to be at once organic, staining as a kind of writing, and architectonic—made of glass, pages as doors. Does he know what he's doing? A detached view of the whole (the Dandy's eye view, masterful and uninvolved) from the point of view of, often, the child (the infant, seeing the adult world from outside, the mastery of innocence). A reconciliation, through a kind of (symbolic) regression, of two obviously quite irreconcilable conditions which also might, from either point of view, be no more than two (necessarily pathetic) versions of the same thing?

He knows what he's doing. The necessity of the pathos has to do with poetry's relationship to meaning-production in the world at large. Poetry knows itself to be the guardian of language and, in that, language's archivist: the ultimately adult language, and in that language at its most uninvolved, "useless." It also knows itself to be where language can play, quite without reference to the reality principle: the ultimately infantile language, once again, language at its most uninvolved. Even in that very narrow world which is not the world at large, the art world, one meets art critics who themselves write that scarcely grammatical form of German-English which is, in America, the sign of the academic, and who would benefit tremendously from having to read a bit of poetry every morning, along with the daytime rush report from their stockbroker and the latest Marxist fashion magazine, but who will in practice airily dismiss poetry as a whole as irrelevant—rather like, one might think, dismissing the unconscious as irrelevant, or suggesting that breathing is irrelevant to speech. In contemporary culture, as I began by saying, poetry is peripheral. It may be described, then, as a form of meaning-production in which uninvolvement meets its own "peripheralization." As such, it is a form which is dandified by default, kept outside whether or not it wants to keep *itself* outside.

Which brings one, I think, to the third and conceivably most important of Shapiro's historico-mythical worlds—the third and a half, inasmuch as I began with a half, a world too narrow to be full (how could it be more than half a world if it couldn't be anything but full?), the world of a particular style or school.

The third and a half world is the one that Shapiro has invented for himself. Geographically, its borders encompass both Passaic and

Prague, linguistically it is prone to dialects, a result of its inhabitants being conversant with both Ovid and Percy Sledge. It is a world produced by the complete internationalization of English which is perhaps one of the great achievements of this century's political contradictions. In Shapiro's world Franz Kafka is a central figure in a literature which may not be English—that is, it may be American—but which is conceived and written in English.

I don't think one is being pedantic in stressing such a point. Some of Shapiro's funniest stuff has to do with the arbitrariness of language, and while that would be true of a lot, if not all, poets in a general sort of way, here it hinges most often on the nonrelationship of words to things, and this becomes, I think, a further articulation of the relationship of poetry to power, which is to say, a relationship of ineffectuality and peripheralization, but an articulation where this relationship is, as it were, reversed by concentrating on the immense power, which is the power of ambiguity, that poetry has over mere power at the symbolic level, confirming the general premise that power has an easier time with things and people than with ideas and signs. An earlier work, before *House (Blown Apart)*, does this in a number of ways. In the following fragment, it does it, first, by taking power away from violence and giving to the grammarian and, second, by giving summative authority to the negative word, the phoneme "no" which stands for no thing and which can negate anything including all not-things, and itself:

> Forget it just become conscious
> think about thinking Just think about it
> What you're doing is an umbrella
> I'm going to push your face in That's a cliché
> Not a ceiling, not a floor . . .
>
> The shadow of the no is on the no
> Maybe the afterimage of the shadow of a no
> Do you think if the Erectheum cannot last
> then this no will last? No
>   "Sphinx Skin" (*TI* 20, 21)

Which is to say that Shapiro's third and a half world, however physically and historically expansive its boundaries might be, is nonetheless a world pressed by, and at the same time mobilized by, the concept of what can't be contained. It is a state wholly at the mercy of the nomads who pass through it at will, to borrow an image from Gilles Deleuze, and steadfastly do no work. Works made out of words both make and undo the world made out of work. We live in a culture entirely devoted to the concept of subversion and the term is therefore difficult to use, but insofar as it retains any operative as opposed to incantatory meaning, one would apply it to Shapiro's poetry and say that what one finds there is the persistent subversion of seriousness by seriousness—the seriousness of the archivist who knows what words mean, the seriousness of the infant building the entire world not from scratch, but from scraps.

Shapiro is quite prepared to use the word "humanist" to describe himself, and the thinkers to whom he will refer, outside of poetry and the poetic, are most often contemporary humanist thinkers not of one sort but, interestingly, sort of one generation: Hannah Arendt, E. M. Forster, Meyer Schapiro, Gershom Scholem. Any general tendency to deploy the grandfathers to overcome father which might be demonstrated by or implicitly in such a list as this, is further manifested in the poetry itself, and is one of its main strengths. Whether or not Shapiro is a humanist in the way that it was perhaps once possible to be (when we had Freud but not yet Lacan, when Marx may have become Stalin but had not yet become Pol Pot or Daniel Ortega, before the inhumanity of Baudrillard's semiology had gobbled up the alienation so nourishing to Adorno's), what sets his poetry apart from so much that is written by others is its complete lack of either knowingness or *naïveté*. It is quite without the slickness which characterizes so much New York poetry, sure as it is of the common assumptions of its audience, the privileged role within it of certain themes—or perhaps only one: the psychology, as far as that can be articulated through poesis, of the very sensitive and at the same time *either* very weary or very self-absorbed. One could say, both positively and negatively, that Shapiro uses sophistication to avoid cleverness. Positively, because it is the depth of his archivalist, humanist professor, sense of poetry which pushes the poetry toward substantial rather than trivial themes and forms, making it and us compare itself with Pound, with the total lack of sentimentality of the haiku, with Ovid, with Kafka's predominant idea—perhaps an ideological position—that the ridiculous should make you feel anxious. Negatively because that sophistication, while rarely if ever lapsing into displayed learning, could be said to retain within itself precisely what some of us would find so irritating about Kafka, the very irritating knowingness of those who know that they don't know, the extremely clever child who, in building a world from scraps, not only keeps asking questions but also coming up with quite brilliant *definitions*—which is to say, de-definitions. Irritation-arousal would become a negative component when it threatened to become formulaic, and the brilliant child playing in a world made out of anxiety threatens to be an image encumbered by nostalgia and its own transparent identity as a familiar mechanism: mastery, even that of the brilliant player as opposed to the profound worker, is always not only mastery over the machinery of illusion but an illusion itself. And we know that and about being anxious about that.

Shapiro's career, thus far, has been prolific and extremely consistent. At its best, which it usually is, his work is extremely dense, in terms of intertextuality, but very supple, or perhaps more exactly, fluid, in the sense of a liquidity rather than a musculature. There are a good number of long poems, and in these, which are, usually the most ambitious works, one, again, usually, finds oneself reading poetry which is quite artless. That is to say, it is absolutely art full without being arch. At its best, Shapiro's poetry is very learned but in a way that defies connoisseurship, like a white painting or a very ambitious classical composition which finds its ambition in eschewing the melody. Shapiro invites comparison with artists like Ryman or Beethoven, with the idea of great ambition.

Which returns once again to poetry's peripheralization. What Shapiro's poetry possesses, and so much else that I read seems to lack, is a capacity for excessive mastery combined with excessive playfulness. Perhaps one must return for an instance to the concepts of pathos and anxiety, and say that what has been peripheralized is the idea of great ambition. That would of course be true. In society today it would be a truism that great art was an idea or a thing of the past, and that we made art which did not mean to be great and, of course, was, in that eschewal of greatness through self-consciousness, greater than great: the meek, as it were, and so on. Shapiro is to be praised and prized for having no truck with such sophistry and instead trying, and I should say succeeding, to make poetry topple one kind of reading into another as only it can do. Ovid and Percy Sledge are, of course, immensely similar, both in the economy of their diction and, incidentally, in their tendency to build poems out of declarations of intent which they clearly have no intention of ever carrying out, like living out in the rain. Poetry knows it cannot really be rendered peripheral, and that its problem is not the peripheral status accorded to it by those who ignore it, but that it lives at the center and is the center, a truth inscribed in the epic which, in recording history and being invented (presumably) to do just that, is all but indifferent to historical fact.

Because if turning things and sensations into poetry levels them out, then it does so through poetry's reasserting its own indifference to them, the indifference of a superior force, poetical meter, the machine which plays with sense, the machinery which the senses find themselves *within*, which narrative tries to *sort out*, to overwhelm and control through an order which obviates poetic order, which begins with the elimination of meter, of rhythm, which is to say, of free play freed by a repetition which is not merely that of discourse. Roman Jakobsen, with whom Shapiro conducted a most useful interview, says in his short work on Pushkin, a writer of considerable interest to Shapiro, that: "It is said with admiration that Pushkin appropriated the world's cultural patrimony without prejudice and from all sides and that he learned to borrow from various periods and national cultures in his works. In reality, though, there is not a shade of eclecticism in him; he can be divinely unjust and heedless."[1] How like Shapiro this sounds! We have perhaps no longer any ready access to the concept of divinity, and must say monstrous rather than divine. And to be unjust is too much part of the (wholly moral) language of fashion nowadays and there we therefore substitute the word "irrelevant," or "irresponsible," or "aesthetic," or "esoteric." And heedlessness is also nowadays too familiar a part of the accessories of self-assertion and so that we invert, substituting "responsible"—to, that is, the rhythm that precedes the word, the uncontrollable capacity for meaning possessed by the word and which the concept to which it becomes attached cannot contain, finding itself, therefore, lost in a sea, or other fluidity, of allusion and denotation, lost and found in poetry.

Note

1. Roman Jakobsen, *Pushkin and His Sculptural Myth* (The Hague: Mouton, 1975), 65.

Afterword:
The Night Sky and
to David Shapiro

Joseph Lease

1

HERE IS RALPH WALDO EMERSON GIVING US THE SOURCE: "[N]ATURE, by worthier impulses, has insured the poet's fidelity to his office of announcement and affirming, namely, by the beauty of things, which becomes a new, and higher beauty, when expressed."[1]

And here is Alice Notley giving us the source of belief: "I find out everything I believe through writing."[2]

2

In 1995 Donald Revell described a new kind of poetic narrativity in the poetry of David Shapiro: "Justly mistrustful of causality and causality's totalizing proportions, the innovators of contemporary poetry abandoned narrative, establishing indeterminacy as the pretext for any subsequent innovations. Yet it now seems to me abandonment has prepared a new place for a new kind of poetic narrativity in which the pressure to tell finds release in the form of a further impulse, inscribing upon quickly distorted syntax a close and quickening tale."[3]

I would like to place David Shapiro in a tradition of prayer, elegy, litany, and sincerity. These are the measures destined for his truth. And he enacts them in a "quickening tale" of lyric structure as dramatic action.

I began studying with David Shapiro in 1978. He electrified me, and he inspired me to explore a different sense of narrative power.

To me his work came to mean that a poem can be a construct of words (actions)—a roller-coaster ride, not a description of a roller-coaster ride. And the poem starts with the abandonment of dead stories in order to make narrative new (or even true).

When I first read Shapiro's amazing "The Night Sky and To Walter Benjamin" I was immediately certain: the poem is both a psalm (a kind of love poem) and an uncanny, evocative ritual celebrating spiritual and intellectual work (poetics).

> Best to use a dead and nervous language
> The extraordinary effort will do nothing
> The sun is so close to us
> The moon of Pluto even the newspaper's moon of Pluto
> so far away
> The one thing Hamlet did not mention
> is that things might get better
> In the clear sea a little glass pulverized for my pleasure
> You do your griefwork, dreamwork, like homework
> Someone lost his money in the night sky
> Someone cut into the shape of dice
> threw the dice against unbounded odds
> light from falling dice.
>
> *(TI* 93)

Lyric structure and poetic language become dramatic action. The poem answers the double impulse to represent and not to represent—that's one of the reasons the poem can enact making (so powerfully and evocatively).

The poem needs to represent the world and the work, and it needs to refuse to represent the world and the work falsely. The pressure to tell drives the making, as does the refusal to be lenient with history, to settle for anything less than an inclusive poetics.

The "further impulse" means that the pressure to tell issues in a new response to multiple traditions and genres. I have always loved this poem, and Poetry is alive and new if we create the music and the self-consciousness and the courage to make stories actual.

3

Donald Revell said recognition is the opposite of seeing. "Morning is when I am awake and there is dawn in me" (Thoreau)[4], and think of Shlovsky's "making strange" and this idea from Charles Bernstein:[5]

> Vendler says
> she hopes readers will be provoked by some of the
> anthologized poems to say—"'Heavens, I recognize
> the place, I know it!' It is the effect every poet
> hopes for. . . . I would hope
> readers might be provoked to say of some poems,
> "Hell, I don't recognize the place or the time or
> the 'I' in this sentence. I don't know it."
> Oh well. (*Artifice of Absorption*)

Let's name that sincerity.

4

Before I met David Shapiro, I was in Evanston, Illinois, with all that snow and all that silence, and I listened to all that snow and all that silence and wrote the most powerful stories I could hear and then I heard the same thing over and over: "Beautiful images . . . but I don't get what you're trying to say."

I began to think of "story" as the oppressor. Tell us what we already know. Don't make us think. Don't make us the slightest bit uncomfortable (good-bye, catharsis).

Shapiro's poems resist conventional ideas about writing and conventional ideas about power. They are tremendously radical and inventive; they are also deeply traditional.

A "traditional" poem constructs a full and supple relationship between language and genre (as source, an ever-changing tale), narrative and abstraction.

Music enacts the passion of transformation—definition, refusal, seeing—in Shapiro's language. These lines come from his elegy for John Cage:

> 33"
> a car because the snow is noiseless
>   different cars (defiant)
> Your light voice in light snow
> elevator without music
>   . . .

> 2' 40"
> Many things are funny
> but this isn't—
> the light snow Thoreau black branches
> protecting the earth by
> such theatrical gestures
> small as a wristwatch.
>
> <div align="right">(<i>BI</i> 29,31)</div>

Cage means, among other wonderful things, attention. Attention to silences and gaps and stillness, and simultaneity.

5

I trust sincerity will not disappear, and, even when I was most distrustful of New York School whimsy, trust in a future for sincerity has always been part of my conversation with David Shapiro. [It goes without saying, but I'll say this as well: I also love camp, goofy irony, breathless irony, unappeasable (ironic) anger, and so on. All forms (nuances) of lyric pleasure. (I guess I mean pleasure and danger. Do I?)]

I mean—look—of course earnestness can destroy (or just damage) a poem—so can glibness, or the cliché of smug (unearned) distance. The opposite of sincerity is not abstraction or constructivism or self-consciousness (self-indictment, contradiction).

When I interviewed David in 1990, I was moved by the way he shifted his poetics away from standard notions of New York School irony and whimsy toward, as he put it, a mode "less lenient with history"; I asked David how he had tried to do this, and here is how he answered me:[6]

> I was always interested in doing a philosophical epic and I continued in *House (Blown Apart)*, *To An Idea*, and in some of my other poems, such as "About this Course" and "Man Holding an Acoustic Panel" to create a sort of elegy to an America I despised. I had an anti-imperialistic theme, politically, that was very difficult to match with monochrome and I was less taken with camp than with Jewish earnestness and with prophetic qualities in Isaiah that were my first sense of poetry. There's a part of me—comically enough, and not everyone might see this—that even links to my old Newark friend Allen Gins-

berg. There is an aspect of my poetry which irked the parodistic in poets such as Ron Padgett and Ted Berrigan, the part of me that's perhaps too involved with seriousness. But I was very taken with the idea of Rilke that one should not be merely ironic and I always told my students to dig past mere irony.

Not that I was involved with confession, but I was very interested (since my wife is an architect and we've lived together for so many years) in structure, in the kind of moral seriousness that you get in the great visionary architecture of John Hejduk, his penological cities, his analogous cities. Aldo Rossi's dream cities might seem to be an analogue, but John's are even more austere. That's why I put John on my cover (of *House (Blown Apart)*). I've been interested in achieving the kind of depressing, massive sense of melancholy that one gets again and again in Jasper Johns (in many ways my aesthetic standard) and the mania for prophetic structures in John Hejduk's great imaginary cities. And I often dream of a poem that will be as labyrinthine as one of John's analogous cities.

That's all very far from the single lament. Jeremy Gilbert-Rolfe said to me that our theme together, as colleagues, painters and poets, is multiplicity. He sees it as Deleuzean. I don't know if that's true but it seems to be one way in which my poetry is more 'demobilized' and 'nomadic' than one might think.

To indicate (sound) the fullness of Shapiro's sincerity in "A Burning Interior," I will quote all of the concluding lyric—"Prayer For A House" (Shapiro's blessing on the visionary architect John Hejduk):

> Blessed is the architect of the removed structures
> Blessed is the structure that weathers in spring snow like lies
> Blessed is the crystal that leaps out of the matrix like a fool
> And blessed is the school
>
> Blessed factures
> Blessed like spring snow
> Blessed like a fool
> And burnt book
>
> Is the school or structure or weather
> Or a lie like spring snow
> And is the matrix leaping also like a fool
> And is the book built or burnt?

> Blessed is the removed
> Blessed too the inlay like spring
> Blessed is the tiger of the matrix like a found fool
> And blessed the unbuilt like a book
>
> Blessed is the architect who survives all removal
> Blessed is the trapped structure like a gift
> Blessed is the crystal fool
> And blessed is the school
>
> Blessed is the cut and the cry
> Blessed is the body of the patient in spring snow like lies
> Blessed is the crystal stepping out of the matrix like a fool
> And blessed is a burning book
>
> Blessed is the anchorite and the architect in the dark smudge
> Blessed is the remover bending to remove
> Blessed is the folly leaping out of matrix
> And blessed is the empty center
>
> Blessed burning structures
> Blessed like snowy spring
> Blessed cry blessed in the matrix like a cut fool
> And blessed each unlit book
>
> Blessed is the architect of the removed cut
> Blessed the structures that weather in lies like spring snow
> Blessed is the crystal that leaps out of the matrix like a fool
> And blessed is the school, like a burning library
>
> Old new prayer
> Old new song
> Blessed is the crystal and the cry and the matrix like a
>   painting fool
> And blessed is the school.
>
> (*BI* 17–18)

Yes, repetition and variation astonish me here; yes, lyric structure becomes dramatic action; yes, repetition and variation enact and continue sincerity (prayer, spell, litany, chant, lament, game). The word school is not the most sincere word in the passage, but it isn't the least sincere either. Shapiro's light touch—his welcoming humor—

graciously acknowledges that you (also) know how high the stakes are.

6

And in a recent issue of PMLA Susan Rubin Suleiman describes Susan Sontag's sincerity: "Asked . . . to define her conception of the intellectual's task, [Sontag] writes . . . that it is twofold: on the one hand, to promote dialogue, skepticism about received ideas, and resistance to nationalist or tribal ideas masquerading as 'ideals'; on the other hand to refuse the facile discrediting of 'idealism,' of altruism itself; of high standards of all kinds."[7]

Refuse the facile discrediting. Doing that requires a process of imagination that never ends, and sincerity. Sontag's version of intellectual work, like Shapiro's, provokes an open-ended questioning.

How many post-language poets in 2005 take Dickinson literally—I mean at her word? I am not sure what the answer is to that, and I'm not sure what the answer should be. Maybe the answer is: we all do take Dickinson literally, but we do it privately. That is the John Kerry answer, I suppose: I'm sincere about spirituality, and you know that because I will not tell you I'm sincere about spirituality. In any case, I don't think we had better leave contested and shimmering words like soul to Robert Bly and the other translators of Rumi. And here is Alice Notley again:[8] "I find out everything I believe through writing. Most of my significant experiences, and most of the things I 'realize' are found out through the practice of poetry, specifically during the performance, the literal writing of it."

7

Shapiro's poems embody musical grace—the distance between grace and death opens new ground for writing.

> Sarcophagus for the still small voice
> Sarcophagus for the marriage of truth and troth
> Sarcophagus for the mother of the hypocritical poet
> Sarcophagus for the lava of speech
>   The incline of music
> Sarcophagus for the materials for the messiah without melancholy.
>   (*BI* 51)

In a new poem, "Subject: A Song," Shapiro gently answers and names our worries about the possibility of making and gives us his poetics. The distance between grace and impossibility opens the ground for awareness. He starts with a sentence by Kant (and with the notion of the human as source)—"Out of the crooked timbre of humanity, no straight thing was ever made"—and he writes and the poem dances:[9]

> Out of Venetian blinds and dream-catchers, out of dreams of Lichtenberg and the desire of Art History, out of wars and branches, out of shadows of my fingers and your hand, out of your riveting nipples and her weightless eyes, out of rockets and buttons, out of the number 5 and out of a red rhino, out of mustaches and Mona Lisas, out of black numbers, nothing straight has ever been made.
>
> Out of colored sand and autumnal trophies, out of chaos and beds, out of a crooked woman and the straight edge of a crystal, out of jade and dust, out of mankind's poor penis and the archaic song of sacrifice, out of Pluto, Medea, and Goofy, out of black boots and Van Gogh's shoes, out of a battered self-portraiture, nothing straight has ever been made.

"Subject: A Song" indicates a kind of meaning grounded in the refusal of conventional certainty. Shapiro's language moves intuitively (wide-awake intuition) in a stream of traditions and awareness made actual.

This should go without saying: his poems raise questions, unsettle conventional notions of closure, and indicate a graceful closure that reimagines closure. The end of this poem—of any given poem—is the start of the transformation Shapiro's work enacts.

8

To see the place in a fresh way—as if for the first time (not to recognize it)—to make the place new—again—when you make it actual in a construct of words. Walter Benjamin on Kafka:[10]

> Just as this bell, which is too loud for a doorbell, rings out toward Heaven, the gestures of Kafka's figures are too powerful for our accustomed surroundings and break out into wider areas. The greater Kafka's mastery became, the more frequently did he eschew adapting these gestures to common situations or explaining them. . . . Like El

Greco, Kafka tears open the sky behind every gesture—but as with El Greco—who was the patron saint of the Expressionists—the gesture remains the decisive thing, the center of the event.... Kafka wished to be numbered among ordinary men. He was pushed to the limits of understanding at every turn, and he liked to push others to them as well.

9

In Shapiro's poems, we are awake and there is dawn in us, and we see the world for the first time, and we renew the sources and powers of poetry that made poets the first lawgivers, the first theologians, the first skeptics, the first tricksters.

David Lehman writes that "Gertrude Stein said that Scott Fitzgerald 'wrote naturally in sentences.' Shapiro writes naturally in poems."[11] That gets it exactly right.

David Shapiro is re-imagining narrative and the lyric self-exploring the texture of involvement, the particulars by which we feel our way in culture and history, and by which we feel culture and history entering our own weave. He is a great and wise and sincere and capacious poet, and poetry is better for it.

Notes

1. Ralph Waldo Emerson, "The Poet," In *Essential Writings* (New York: Modern Library, 2000), 292.
2. Alice Notley, "A Conversation: Claudia Keelan and Alice Notley." In *Interim.* (University of Nevada at Las Vegas: 2005), 122.
3. Donald Revell, Review of *The Room. Colorado Review* 21.2 (fall 1995), 200.
4. Henry David Thoreau, *The Illustrated Walden*, ed. J. Lyndon Shanley (Princeton, NJ: Princeton University Press, 1973), 90.
5. Charles Bernstein, Artifice of Absorption (Philadelphia: Singing Horse Press, 1987), 30-31.
6. Joseph Lease, "After the New York School," Interview with David Shapiro, *Pataphysics Magazine* 1990 http://www.pataphysicsmagazine.com/ shapiro_ interview.html
7. Susan Rubin Suleiman, "Culture, Aestheticism, and Ethics: Sontag and the 'Idea of Europe.'" *PMLA* (May 2005): 841.
8. Alice Notley, 122.
9. David Shapiro, "Subject: A Song." *No* 4 (2005): 59–60.
10. Walter Benjamin, "Franz Kafka on the Tenth Anniversary of his Death" In *Illuminations* (New York: Shocken, 1969), 120–21, 124.
11. David Lehman, jacket copy, David Shapiro, *A Burning Interior.*

Works Cited

Ashbery, John. *Rivers and Mountains*. New York: Holt, Rinehart and Winston, 1967.

———. *As We Know*. New York: Penguin. 1979.

Barbiero, Daniel. "Reflection on Lyric Before, During and After Language." In *The World in Time and Space: Towards a History of Innovative American Poetry in Our Time*. Ed. Edward Foster and Joseph Donahue. Jersey City, NJ: Talisman House, 2002. 355–66.

Bartlett, Lee. *Talking Poetry: Conversations in the Workshop with Contemporary Poets*. Albuquerque: University of New Mexico Press, 1987.

Bassford, Elizabeth. "The Beautiful View: Lunch with David Shapiro." *Exoterica*. (2003) http://www.exoterica.org/shapirointerview.html.

Benjamin, Walter. *Illuminations*. New York: Schocken Books, 1969.

Bernstein, Charles. *Artifice of Absorption*. Philadelphia: Singing Horse Press, 1987.

———. *My Way: Speeches and Poems*. Chicago: University of Chicago Press, 1999.

Bloom, Harold. Review of David Shapiro's *Lateness*. *Saturday Review* (December 1977): 83.

Cage, John. "Jasper Johns: Stories and Ideas." In *The New Art*. Ed. Gregory Battcock. New York: E.P. Dutton, 1966. 219–21.

Denby, Edwin. *Homage to Frank O'Hara*. Eds. Bill Berkson and Joe LeSuer Berkeley: Creative Arts Books, 1980. 30–32.

Emerson, Jocelyn. "An Interview with Jane Miller." *Electronic Poetry Review*, 1 (2002) http://www.poetry.org/issues/issue1/alltext/intmil.htm.

Emerson, Ralph Waldo. *Essential Writings*. New York: Modern Library, 2000.

Fink, Thomas. *The Poetry of David Shapiro*. Rutherford, NJ: Fairleigh Dickinson University Press, 1993.

———. *"A Different Sense of Power": Problems of Community in Late- Twentieth Century U.S. Poetry*. Rutherford, NJ: Fairleigh Dickinson University Press, 2001.

———. "David Shapiro's "Possibilist Poetry.'" *Jacket* 24 (November 2003) http://jacketmagazine.com/24.html.

Fontenelle, Bernard le Bovier. *Conversations on the Plurality of Worlds*. Trans. H. A. Hargreaves. 1686. Berkeley: University of California Press, 1990.

Fuhrman, Joanna. "Pluralist Music: An Interview with David Shapiro." *Rain Taxi Online*. (Fall 2002) http://www.raintaxi.com/online/2002fall/shapiro.shtml.

Gadamer, Hans-Georg. *The Relevance of the Beautiful.* Trans. Nicholas Walker. Cambridge: Cambridge University Press, 1989.

———. *Hans-Georg Gadamer on Education, Poetry, and History.* Ed. Dieter Misgeld and Graeme Nicholson. Trans. Lawrence Schmidt and Monica Reuss. Albany, NY: State University of New York Press, 1992.

———. "Text and Interpretation." *Dialogue and Deconstruction.* Eds. Diane P. Michelfelder and Richard E. Palmer. Albany: State University of New York Press, 1989. 21–51.

———. *Truth and Method.* 2nd rev. ed. Rev. trans. Joel Weinsheimer and Donald G. Marshall. New York: Crossroad, 1990.

Gizzi, Peter. *Artificial Heart.* Providence: Burning Deck, 1998.

———. Interview with Samuel Truitt. 1993. Brown University. http://www.brown.edu/Departments/Literary_Arts/pgizzitruitt.html

———. *Some Values of Landscape and Weather.* Middletown, CT: Wesleyan University Press, 2003.

Gluck, Robert. "Long Note on New Narrative." *Narrativity* 1, nd. http://www.sfsu.edu/~newlit/narrativity/issue_one/gluck.html.

Grossman, Allen. *The Sighted Singer: Two Works on Poetry for Readers and Writers.* Baltimore: Johns Hopkins University Press, 1992.

Haney, David P. "Aesthetics and Ethics in Gadamer, Levinas, and Romanticism: Problems of Phronesis and Techne." *PMLA* 114.1 (January 1999): 32–45.

Hauke, Nathan. "Meditations on David Shapiro: Memory and *Lateness.*" *Jacket 23* (August 2003) http://www.jacketmagazine.com.

Hauser, Arnold. *The Social History of Art.* New York: Routledge, 2003.

Heidegger, Martin. *Being and Time.* Trans. John Macquarrie and Edward Robinson. New York: Harper and Row, 1962.

Hell, Richard and David Shapiro. "IV," *Richard Hell: Official Site,* (2003) www.richardhell.com/IVpoem.html.

Hyde, Lewis. *The Gift: Imagination and the Erotic Life of Property.* New York: Vintage, 1983.

Jakobsen, Roman. *Pushkin and His Sculptural Myth.* The Hague: Mouton, 1975.

Keelan, Claudia and Alice Notley. "A Conversation." *Interim.* University of Nevada at Las Vegas (2005): 119–23.

Koch, Kenneth. *Selected Poems.* New York: Random House, 1985.

Kockelmans, Joseph J. *On the Truth of Being: Reflections on Heidegger's Later Philosophy.* Bloomington: Indiana University Press, 1984.

Kosalka, David. "Georges Bataille and the Notion of Gift." 1999. *The Historian Underground.* http://www.lemmingland.com/bataille.html

Kozloff, Max. *Jasper Johns.* New York: Abrams, 1967.

Lacan, Jacques. *Ecrits.* New York: Norton, 1977.

Lease, Joseph. "After the New York School." Interview with David Shapiro. *Pataphysics Magazine.* 1990. http://www.pataphysicsmagazine.com/shapiro_interview.html

Lingis, Alphonso. *The Community of Those Who Have Nothing in Common.* Bloomington and Indianapolis: Indiana University Press, 1994.

Mauss, Marcel. *The Gift: Forms and Functions of Exchange in Archaic Societies.* New York: Norton, 1967.

Miller, Stephen Paul. Unpublished interview with David Shapiro, October 30, 1981.

Nathanson, Tenney. *Whitman's Presence: Body, Voice, and Writing in Leaves of Grass.* New York: New York University Press, 1992.

O'Hara, Frank. *The Collected Poems of Frank O'Hara.* Ed. Donald Allen. New York: Knopf, 1971.

———. *Lunch Poems.* San Francisco: City Lights, 1964.

Olson, Charles. *Selected Writings of Charles Olson.* Ed. Robert Creeley. New York: Directions, 1966.

Oppen, George. *Selected Poems.* New York: New Directions, 2003.

Palmer, Michael. *First Figure.* San Francisco: North Point Press, 1984.

Perelman, Bob [and Ron Sillman, Barrett Watten, Steve Benson, Lyn Hejinian, Charles Bernstein]. "for *Change*," *In the American Tree.* Ed. Ron Silliman. Orono, ME: National Poetry Foundation, 1986. 484–90.

Poggeler, Otto. *Martin Heidegger's Path of Thinking.* Trans. Daniel Magurshak and Sigmund Barber. Atlantic Highlands, NJ: Humanities Press International, Inc., 1987.

Revell, Donald. Review of *The Room. Colorado Review* 21.2 (fall 1995): 199–209.

Richards, I.A. *The Philosophy of Rhetoric.* 1939. New York: Oxford University Press, 1965.

Ricoeur, Paul. "The Metaphorical Process." In *On Metaphor.* Ed. Sheldon Sacks. Chicago: University of Chicago Press, 1979, 141–58.

Risser, James. *Hermeneutics and the Voice of the Other: Re-reading Gadamer's Philosophical Hermenuetics.* Albany: State University of New York Press, 1997.

Schilder, Paul. *The Image and Appearance of the Human Body.* New York: International Universities Press, 1978.

Shapiro, David. *January.* New York: Holt, Rinehart and Winston, 1965.

———. *Poems from Deal.* New York: E.P. Dutton, 1969.

———. *A Man Holding an Acoustic Panel.* New York: E. P. Dutton, 1971.

———. *The Page-Turner.* New York: Liveright, 1973.

———. *Lateness.* Woodstock, NY: Overlook, 1977.

———. *John Ashbery: An Introduction to the Poetry.* New York: Columbia University Press, 1979.

———. *Poets and Painters: Lines of Color.* Denver: Denver Art Museum, 1979.

———. *To an Idea.* Woodstock, NY: Overlook, 1983.

———. *House (Blown Apart).* Woodstock, NY: Overlook, 1988.

———. *After a Lost Original.* Woodstock, NY: Overlook, 1994.

———. "Mondrian's Secret." In *Uncontrollable Beauty.* Ed. Bill Beckley with David Shapiro. New York: Allworth Press, 1998.

———. *A Burning Interior*. Woodstock, NY: Overlook, 2002.

———. "Subject: A Song." *No* 4 (2005): 59–60.

———. and Stephen Paul Miller. *Harrisburg Mon Amour, or Two Boys On A Bus*. Unpublished typescript. 1979–1980.

Smith, Stevie. *Collected Poems*. New York: Oxford University Press, 1976.

Steinberg, Leo. *Other Criteria*. New York: Oxford University Press, 1972.

Stevens, Wallace. *The Collected Poems*. New York: Knopf, 1977.

———. *The Noble Rider and the Sound of Words*. New York: Vintage Books, 1951.

Stroffolino, Chris. *Spin Cycle*. New York: Spuyten Duyvil, 2001.

Suleiman, Susan Rubin. "Culture, Aestheticism, and Ethics: Sontag and the 'Idea of Europe.'" *PMLA* (May 2005): 839–42.

Sullivan, Gary. "Kevin Killian Interview." *Read Me* 4 (Spring/Summer 2001) *http://home.jps.net/~nada/killian.html*.

Thoreau, Henry David. *The Illustrated Walden*. Ed. J. Lyndon Shanley. Princeton, NJ: Princeton University Press, 1973.

Tomkins, Calvin. *The Bride and the Bachelors*. New York: Penguin Books, 1962.

———. *Robert Rauschenberg and the Art World of Our Time*. New York: Penguin, 1980.

Tranter, John. "David Shapiro in Conversation with John Tranter, New York, 15 February 1984." *Jacket* 23 (August 2003): *http://jacketmagazine.com/23*.

Wachterhauser, Brice R. *Beyond Being: Gadamer's Post-Platonic Hermeneutical Ontology*. Evanston, IL: Northwestern University Press, 1999.

Wallace, Mark. "Definitions in Process/ Definitions as Process/ Uneasy Collaborations: Language and Postlanguage Poetries." *Flashpoint* Web Issue 2 (Spring 1998) *http://www.flashpointmag.com/postlang.html*.

Weil, Simone. *The Simone Weil Reader*. Ed. George A. Panichas. Mt. Kisco, NY: Moyer Bell Limited, 1977.

Whithaus, Carl. "Immediate Memories: (Nostalgic) Time and (Immediate) Loss in the Poetry of David Shapiro." *Rocky Mountain Language Association* (1997) *http://rmmla.wsu.edu/ereview/53.1/articles/Whithaus/asp*.

Williams, William Carlos. *Imaginations*. New York: New Directions, 1970.

Ziarek, Krzysztof. *Inflected Language: Toward a Hermeneutics of Nearness*. Albany: State University of New York Press, 1994.

Contributors

DENISE DUHAMEL, Professor of English at Florida International University, is the author of numerous books and chapbooks of poetry. Her most recent titles are *Two and Two* (2005) and *Queen for a Day: Selected and New Poems* (2001). Her other titles currently in print are *The Star-Spangled Banner*, winner of the Crab Orchard Poetry Prize (1999); *Exquisite Politics* (with Maureen Seaton, 1997); *Kinky* (1997); *Girl Soldier* (1996); and *How the Sky Fell* (1996). A winner of a National Endowment for the Arts Fellowship, she has been anthologized widely, including four volumes of *The Best American Poetry* (2000, 1998, 1994, and 1993).

THOMAS FINK, Professor of English at City University of New York-LaGuardia, is the author of two critical studies published by Fairleigh Dickinson University Press, *The Poetry of David Shapiro* (1993) and *"A Different Sense of Power": Problems of Community in Late-Twentieth-Century U.S. Poetry* (2001). He has also published four books of poetry, including *After Taxes* (2004) and *No Appointment Necessary* (2006). His critical writing has appeared in *Contemporary Literature, Verse, Talisman, American Poetry Review, Jacket, Denver Quarterly, Chicago Review, Minnesota Review, Confrontation, American Book Review, Boston Review*, and numerous other journals. Fink's paintings hang in various collections.

JOANNA FUHRMAN is the author of three collections of poetry published by Hanging Loose Press, *Freud in Brooklyn* (2000), *Ugh Ugh Ocean* (2003) and *Moraine* (2006). Her poems have appeared in many journals and anthologies including *Lit, New American Writing, New York Times, American Letters and Commentary,* and *American Poetry: Next Generation*. She is a graduate of the University of Washington's MFA program, which awarded her the Academy of American Poet's Prize and the Joan Grayson Award. She has taught poetry at the University of Washington and at the Poetry Project at Saint Mark's Church.

JEREMY GILBERT-ROLFE is a critic, painter, and author of several books, including *Beyond Piety: Critical Essays on the Visual Arts 1986–1993* and *Immanence and Contradiction: Recent Essays on the Artistic Device*. He has been awarded National Endowment for the Arts fellowships in painting and criticism as well as a Guggenheim fellowship in painting, and was presented the 1998 Frank Jewett Mather Award for Art Criticism by the College Art Association. He teaches in the graduate program at Art Center College of Design in Pasadena, California.

NOAH ELI GORDON, born in Cleveland, Ohio, in 1975, is the author of two books of poetry, *The Frequencies* (2003) and *The Area of Sound Called the Subtone* (2004). He publishes the Braincase chapbook series. His poetry and reviews have appeared in numerous journals and chapbooks.

JUDITH HALDEN-SULLIVAN, Associate Professor of English at Millersville State University in Millersville, Pennsylvania, is the author of *The Topology of Being: The Poetics of Charles Olson* (1991). She contributed an essay to *Into the Field: The Interdisciplinary Site of Composition Studies* (1993), and has published work in various other journals.

PAUL HOOVER, a Professor in the Creative Writing department at San Francisco State University, is the author of *Poems in Spanish* (2005), *Fables of Representation: Essays* (2004), and nine poetry collections, including *Winter (Mirror)* (2002), *Rehearsal in Black* (2001), *Totem and Shadow: New & Selected Poems* (1999), and *Viridian* (University of Georgia Press, 1997). He has also published a novel, *Saigon, Illinois* (1988), a chapter of which appeared in *New Yorker*. He is the editor of the anthology *Postmodern American Poetry* (1994) and the literary magazine *New American Writing* (with Maxine Chernoff). Hoover has received the Jerome J. Shestack Prize for best poetry published in *American Poetry Review*, 2002, the Carl Sandberg Award for poetry, 1987, the General Electric Foundation Award for Younger Writers, 1984, and an NEA Fellowship in Poetry, 1980.

JOSEPH LEASE is Associate Professor of Writing and Literature at California College of the Arts. His books of poetry include *Broken World* (forthcoming) and *Human Rights*. His poem "'Broken World' (For James Assatly)" was selected by Robert Creeley for *The Best American Poetry 2002*. His poems have also been featured on NPR and published in The *AGNI 30th Anniversary Poetry Anthology*, *Bay Poetics* (forthcoming), *The Boston Review, Colorado Review, Talisman, New American Writing, Grand Street, Paris Review, Volt, Xantippe, Fence, Five Fingers Review, Denver Quarterly*, and elsewhere.

TIMOTHY LIU was born and raised in San José, California. His first book of poems, *Vox Angelica*, received the 1992 Norma Farber First Book Award from the Poetry Society of America. His other books are *Burnt Offerings, Say Goodnight, Hard Evidence* (2001), *Of Thee I Sing* (2004), selected as a 2004 Book of the Year by *Publishers Weekly*, and *For Dust Thou Art* (2005). His journals and papers are archived in the Berg Collection at the New York Public Library. An Associate Professor of English at William Paterson College and a member of the Core Faculty in Bennington College's Writing Seminars, Liu is the editor of *Word of Mouth: An Anthology of Gay American Poetry* (2000).

STEPHEN PAUL MILLER, Professor of English at St. John's University, is the author of *The Seventies Now: Culture as Surveillance* (1999) and coeditor of *The Scene of My Selves: New Work On New York School Poets* (National Poetry Foundation, 2001). He has published three books of poetry, *Skinny Eighth Avenue* (2005), *The Bee Flies In May* (2002), and *Art Is Boring for the Same Reason We Stayed in Vietnam* (1992), as well as several chapbooks. His work as appeared in *Best American Poetry* 1994, *boundary* 2, *Talisman, Shofar, American Letters & Commentary, Poetry New York, St. Marks Poetry Project Newsletter, Sagetrieb, Mudfish, La Petite Zine, Scripsi, Proteus*, and elsewhere. He has had gallery shows at PS1 and William Paterson College's Ben Shawn Gallery in New York City.

DANIEL MORRIS, Professor of English at Purdue University, is the author of *The Writings of William Carlos Williams: Publicity for the Self* (1995), *Remarkable Modernisms: Contemporary American Authors on Modern Art* (2002), and *Bryce Passage* (2004), a book of poems. He has also edited or coedited two collections of essays: one on the Jewish-American poet Allen Grossman (2004), and a second on the legacy of the

New York Jewish Public Intellectuals (forthcoming). His book-length study of the Jewish-American author Louise Glück is forthcoming. He is editor of *Shofar*, an interdisciplinary journal of Jewish studies.

TIM PETERSON's chapbooks are *Cumulus* and *Trinkets Mashed into a Blender*. His poetry and criticism have been published or are forthcoming in *Antennae, artsMEDIA, Colorado Review, EOAGH, Harvard Review, Leonardo Electronic Almanac, POG3, The Poker, Rain Taxi, Transgender Tapestry*, and *VeRT*. He currently edits the journal *EOAGH*.

RON SILLIMAN has written and edited twenty-five books to date, most recently *Woundwood*. Between 1979 and 2004, Silliman wrote a single poem entitled *The Alphabet*. In addition to *Woundwood*, a part of VOG, volumes published thus far from that project have included *ABC, Demo to Ink, Jones, Lit, Manifest, N/O, Paradise, (R), Toner, What*, and *Xing*. He is the editor of the anthology *In the American Tree* and the author of the critical book, *The New Sentence*. Silliman was a 2003 Literary fellow of the National Endowment for the Arts and was a 2002 Fellow of the Pennsylvania Arts Council as well as a Pew Fellow in the Arts in 1998. He lives in Chester County, Pennsylvania, with his wife and two sons, and works as a market analyst in the computer industry.

CAROLE STONE is Professor Emeritus of English at Montclair State University in New Jersey. Her most recent books of poetry are: *Vinegar and Salt, Orphan in the Movie House*, and *Lime and Salt*. She received three Fellowships in Poetry from the New Jersey State Council on the Arts, a Fellowship from the Geraldine Dodge Foundation, a Fellowship from Hawthornden Castle Writers Retreat in Scotland and Chateau Lavigny in Switzerland. Her poems have appeared in *The Beloit Poetry Journal, Chelsea, Southern Poetry Review*, and *Nimrod International Poetry Journal*. In the United Kingdom her work has appeared in *The North, Nottingham International Poetry Journal, Orbis*, and *Smiths Knoll*.

Index

Abstract Expressionism, 69, 71, 87 n. 5
Achilles, 89, 139
Alcestis, 113
Anderson, Laurie, 97 n. 6, 124
Andrews, Bruce, 123
Arendt, Hannah, 19, 160
Ashbery, John, 19, 28, 30, 32, 60, 61, 69, 70, 72, 74, 87 n. 5, 88, 89, 90, 91, 102, 123, 134, 139, 140, 141, 142, 156; "A Blessing in Disguise," 28; *As We Know,* 97 n. 5 ; "Litany," 90; *Rivers and Mountains,* 28, 30 n. 9; *Self-Portrait in a Convex Mirror,* 23, 123; *The Tennis Court Oath,* 123, 136 n. 3

Barbiero, Daniel, 13, 20 n. 2
Bassford, Elizabeth, 98; "The Beautiful View," 106 n. 1, 136 n. 3
Bataille, Georges, 109, 116 n. 9
Baudelaire, Charles, 87 n. 5
Baudrillard, Jean, 160
Beethoven, Ludwig Van, 155, 160
Bellamy, Dodie, 125
Benjamin, Walter, 20, 21, 170–71; *Illuminations,* 30 n.1, 109, 116 n. 6, 171 n. 10
Benson, Steve, 124
Bernstein, Charles, 13, 124, 127, 137 n. 12, 165; *Artifice of Absorption,* 171 n. 5; *My Way,* 20 n. 1, 29
Berrigan, Ted, 117, 167
Berssenbrugge, Mei-mei, 23, 136 n. 10
The Best American Poetry, 14

Black Mountain School, 13, 137 n. 12
Bloom, Harold, 14, 72, 112
Bly, Robert, 169
Boone, Bruce, 125
Borges, Jorge Luis, 98
Brainard, Joe, 117
Brakhage, Stan, 108
Brathwaite, Kamau, 137 n. 12
Broumas, Olga, 104–5
Browning, Elizabeth Barrett, 28
Bruno, Giordano, 23
Bush, George, 131
Bush, George W., 117

Cabri, Louis: *The Mood Embosser,* 117
Cage, John, 16, 20, 22, 75, 76, 77, 84, 85, 91, 124, 165, 166; *Suite for Toy Piano,* 22; "Jasper Johns: Stories and Ideas," 87 n. 23
Caesar, Julius, 91, 93
Carroll, Lewis: *Alice in Wonderland,* 100, 104
Carter, Eliot, 124
Cavafy, C. P.: "The First Step," 52
Ceravolo, Joseph, 55–56, 124
Cezanne, Paul, 111
Chagall, Marc, 63
Chekhov, Anton, 92, 93
The China Syndrome, 94–95
Codrescu, Andrei, 14
Collaborative Poetry, 17, 98–106
Columbia University, 18, 88, 95, 117, 123, 130
Coolidge, Clark, 124

Corrie, Rachel, 121
Creeley, Robert, 14
Cubism, 77–78

de Kooning, Willem, 69, 74, 91, 112
de Man, Paul, 123
Deleuze, Gilles, 160, 167
Deleuze and Felix Guattari, 144
Demeter, 113
Denby, Edwin, 69; *Homage to Frank O'Hara*, 86 n. 2
Derrida, Jacques, 90, 123, 147
Dickinson, Emily, 169
Donahue, Joseph, 20, 136 n. 10
Dubuffet, Jean, 71
Duhamel, Denise, 16, 17, 98–106, 177

Eliot, T. S., 19, 91, 124, 156
Elmslie, Kenward, 69
Eluard, Paul, 145
Emerson, Jocelyn: "An Interview with Jane Miller," 106 n. 7
Emerson, Ralph Waldo, 20, 163; "The Poet," 171 n. 1

Ferlinghetti, Lawrence, 120
Fink, Thomas, 13, 18, 31, 32, 34, 37, 61, 68 nn. 3 and 4, 99, 123–37, 143–44, 177; "David Shapiro's 'Possibilist' Poetry," 45 nn. 2, 6, and 13, 106 n. 2; "*A Different Sense of Power*," 136 n. 7; *The Poetry of David Shapiro*, 18, 34, 45 nn. 9 and 14, 137 n. 12, 149, 150 n. 5, 151 n. 11
Fitzgerald, F. Scott, 171
Fontenelle, Bernard, 23, 30 n. 4
Foster, Edward, 20
Forster, E. M., 160
Foucault, Michel, 155
Free Speech Movement, 118
Freud, Sigmund, 145, 146, 157, 160
Fuhrman, Joanna, 15, 16, 17, 29, 47–59, 101, 177; "Pluralist Music: An Interview with David Shapiro," 29, 30 nn. 10 and 11, 68 n. 2 and 5, 106 n. 3, 109–10, 116 n. 12, 121, 130, 136 n. 3

Gadamer, Hans-Georg, 15, 31–32, 34, 36–37, 39–40, 43, 44, 45; "On the Contribution of Poetry to the Search for Truth," 31, 45 nn. 3, 10, 11, 12, 19, and 20; 46 nn. 31 and 32; "The Relevance of the Beautiful," 45 n. 18; "Text and Interpretation," 46 n. 21; *Truth and Method*, 46 n. 30
Gilbert-Rolfe, Jeremy, 18, 19, 154–62, 167, 178
Gilgamesh, 89
Ginsberg, Allen, 60, 61, 62; *Kaddish*, 61, 166–67
Gizzi, Peter, 17, 107, 111–12, 115, 116 n. 19; Interview with Sam Truitt, 116 n. 17; "Rewriting the Other and the Others," 112, 113–14, 116 n. 21 and 22; *Some Values of Landscape and Weather*, 116 n. 25
Gluck, Robert: "Long Note on New Narrative," 125–26, 136 n. 6, 7, and 8
Goddard, Jean Luc, 90
Gordon, Noah Eli, 117, 107–16, 178
Gregory, André, 95
Grossman, Allen, 89; *The Sighted Singer*, 97 nn. 1, 2, and 3
Guest, Barbara, 23, 69; "Wild Gardens Overlooked by Night Lights," 23

Halden-Sullivan, Judith, 15, 16, 17, 19, 31–46, 178
Haney, David, 40, 43; "Aesthetics and Ethics in Gadamer, Levinas, and Romanticism," 46 nn. 22, 26, 27, and 28
Harryman, Carla, 125
Hauser, Arnold, 19, 142, 145, 149; *The Social History of Art*, 150 n. 4, 151 nn. 8 and 13
Hauke, Nathan, 32; "Meditations on David Shapiro: Memory and *Lateness*," 45 n. 5
Heidegger, Martin, 32, 37, 40; *Being and Time*, 45 n. 4
Heisenberg, Werner, 35

Hejduk, John, 18, 121, 167
Hejinian, Lyn, 14, 124
Hell, Richard, 104, 106 nn. 5 and 6
Hiroshima mon amour, 94
Holderlin, Friedrich, 15, 25, 29
Homer, 68
Hoover, Paul, 15, 19, 21–30, 178
Hugo, Victor, 51
Hussein, Saddam, 131
Husserl, Edmund, 147
Hyde, Lewis, 17, 115; *The Gift*, 109, 116 n. 7, 8, and 23

I Ching, 76
The Iliad, 89

Jakobsen, Roman, 70, 162; *Pushkin and His Sculptural Myth*, 162 n. 1
Johns, Jasper, 16, 29, 69, 71, 72, 74, 77–78, 79–80, 81, 82, 83–85, 86, 87 n. 5, 124, 167; "*In the Studio*," 85; *False Start*, 79; *Flag* paintings, 77, 79, 83; *Target with Four Faces*, 79, 84
Joron, Andrew, 136 n. 10

Kafka, Franz, 20, 159, 160, 161, 170–71
Kant, Immanuel, 170
Katz, Alex, 88
Keats, John, 27, 63
Kerry, John, 169
Killian, Kevin, 125, 136 n. 8
Kilmister, Clive, 79
Kirk, Grayson, 18
Kissinger, Henry, 57
Klee, Paul, 48
Koch, Kenneth, 28, 30 n.8, 60, 70, 72, 73, 87 n. 5, 88, 136 n. 3; "To You," 28
Kockelmans, Joseph: *On the Truth of Being*, 46 n. 24
Kosalka, David: "Georges Bataille and the Notion of Gift," 116 n. 9
Kozloff, Max, 83; *Jasper Johns*, 87 n. 21

Lacan, Jacques, 19, 123, 144, 151 n. 7, 160

Language Poetry, 13, 18, 19, 21, 70, 86, 107, 123–25, 126–27
Lauterbach, Ann, 136 n. 10
Lease, Joseph, 13, 14, 19–20, 136 n. 10, 163–71, 179; "After the New York School," 14, 20, 116 n. 11, 126, 132, 135, 136 n. 3, 166–67; 171 n. 6
Lehman, David, 14, 171
Levertov, Denise, 120
Life, 17, 118, 130
Lingis, Alphonso, 108–9, 111; "The Murmur of the World," 108–9; 116 nn. 5 and 18
Liu, Timothy: "For Dust Thou Art," 19, 152–53, 179
Louis, Morris: *Veils*, 71
Lowell, Robert, 89

Mackey, Nathaniel, 137 n. 12
Mallarmé, Stephane, 19, 22, 33, 123, 155, 158
Mannerism, 19, 139–40, 141, 142
Marker, Chris, 108
Marx, Karl, 160
Mauss, Marcel, 17, 109
McLuhan, Marshall, 78
Mead, Taylor, 92–93
Michelson, Albert and Edward Morley, 120
Miller, Jane, 104–5
Miller, Stephen Paul, 16, 69–87, 88–97, 105, 137 n. 10, 179
Mondrian, Piet, 29
Moore, Marianne, 121
Morris, Daniel, 16–17, 88–97, 179–80
Mozart, Wolfgang Amadeus, 91, 92, 93
My Dinner with Andre, 94, 95

Nathanson, Tenney, 19, 146–7, 150 n. 6, 151 n. 9
New Narrative, 18, 125–26
The New Sentence, 23
New York School (of Poetry), 13, 14, 15, 16, 17, 22, 28, 60, 69–70, 71, 85, 86 n. 5, 88, 91, 98, 117, 121, 123, 124, 137 n. 12, 156, 166

New York School (of Painting), 69–70, 71, 85
Notley, Alice, 117–118, 163, 169; "A Conversation," 171 nn. 2 and 8

Objectivism, 137 n. 12
O'Hara, Frank, 14, 29, 60, 61, 66, 69, 72, 73, 78, 87 n. 5, 156; "Adieu to Norman, Bonjour to Joan and Jean-Paul," 72
Olson, Charles, 33, 39, 42; *Selected Writings*, 45 nn. 7 and 17; *The Special View of History*, 46 n. 25
Oppen, George, 22, 30 nn. 2 and 3
Orpheus, 113
Ortega, Daniel, 160
Ovid, 159, 160, 161–62

Padgett, Ron, 167
Palach, Jan, 18, 120
Palmer, Michael, 14, 17, 21, 107, 108, 109, 110, 113, 115, 116 n. 13; "Music Rewritten," 108, 115, 116 nn. 3, 4, and 24
Parmagianino, 19; *Self-Portrait in a Convex Mirror*, 23
Perelman, Bob: "For Change," 124–25, 127, 136 nn. 4 and 5, 137 n. 12
Persephone, 112–13
Peterson, Tim, 15, 18–19, 138–51, 180
Petlin, Irving, 130
Plato, 48, 54
Poggeler, Otto, 39, 45 n. 16
Pol Pot, 160
Pollock, Jackson, 69, 71, 74, 110
Post-Language Poetry, 18, 126–27, 137 n. 12, 169
Postmodernism, 15, 22, 44
Pound, Ezra, 19, 70, 156
Proust, Marcel, 123
Pushkin, Aleksandr, 51, 162

Rauschenberg, Robert, 71, 72, 74; 87 n. 5, 112, 124; *White Painting with Numbers*, 71
Reeves, Keanu, 94
Resnais, Alain, 94

Revell, Donald, 163, 164, 171 n. 3
Rich, Adrienne, 14
Richards, I. A.: *The Philosophy of Rhetoric*, 138, 150 n. 1
Ricouer, Paul, 149–50, 151 n. 12
Rimbaud, Arthur, 91, 115 n. 1
Risser, James: *Hermeneutics and the Voice of the Other*, 45 n. 1, 46 n. 35.
Rivers, Larry, 69, 87 n. 5, 88
Robbe-Grillet, 27; *Jalousie*, 27
Rossi, Aldo, 167
Roussel, Raymond, 19, 139
Rumi, 169
Ryman, Robert, 160

San Francisco Renaissance, 13, 137 n. 12
Santayana, George, 91
Sappho, 22
Schapiro, Meyer, 19, 110, 111, 130, 160
Schilder, Paul: *The Image and Appearance of the Body*, 147, 151 n. 10
Schjeldahl, Peter, 117
Scholem, Gershom, 160
Schuyler, James, 14, 55, 69, 70
SDS (Students for a Democratic Society), 118
Seaton, Peter, 125
Shapiro, Daniel, 50, 51, 98–102
Shapiro, David:
—Works: "About a Farmer Who Was Just a Little Boy," 103–4; "About this Course," 166; *After a Lost Original* 15, 21–27, 39, 52, 53, 66, 98, 110, 115, 138; "After a Lost Original," 50, 53–55, 110; "After *Asturiana*," 23–25, 37, 40–41; "An Afternoon with a Lion," 73–74, 147–48; *An Anthology of New York Poets*, 117, 122 n. 1; "Another Marschallin," 155; "Archaic Torsos," 36 ; "Art as Collaboration: Toward a Theory of Pluralist Aesthetics," 16; "A Book of Doors," 156; "Black Silk," 98, 101; "The Blank Wall," 36 ; "The Boss Poem," 98, 99–100; *A Burning Inte-*

rior, 18, 36, 48, 50, 110, 127, 131; "A Burning Interior," 51; "Canticle," 78, 79; "The Car in a Maze," 98, 101; "Cheap Elegy for John," 165–66; "The Counter-Example," 145; "Christ in Prague," 131; "The Cup in Architecture," 31, 35–36; "Dante and Beatrice (at Forty-Seven), 57; "The Destruction of the Bulwarks at Deal," 67; "The Devil's Trill Sonata," 72–73, 82, 124, 146; "Doubting the Doubts," 32; "Drawing After Summer," 115; "Dream of December Ninth," 131; "Elegy to Sports," 66; "An Example of Work," 114; "An Exercise in Futility," 75–76, 143; "Falling Upwards," 28–29; "A Family Slide," 80–81; "A Found Golf Ball," 57–58; "For the Evening Land," 131; "The Funeral of Jan Palach," 18, 120–21; "God Meets the Angel," 98, 99, 101, 102; "God's Shadow," 98, 101–2; *Harrisburg, Mon Amour, or Two Boys on a Bus*, 16, 88–97; "The Heavenly Humor," 34, 124; "House," 39, 41, 66; "House (IV)," 156; *House (Blown Apart)*," 15, 34–36, 49, 110, 114, 159, 166; "House (Blown Apart), 34–36, 110, 149; "House of the Secret," 52–53, 115; "In Germany," 25; "In Memory of Goofy," 50–51, 53; "In Memory of Poetry," 157; "In Memory of Your Body," 63–64, 66; "IV," 104; *January* 87 n. 5, 118; *John Ashbery: An Introduction to the Poetry*, 23, 30 n. 5, 68 n. 1, 110–11, 112, 115 n. 2, 116 n. 14, n. 20, 123, 135 n. 1, 136 n. 2, 139, 150 nn.2 and 3; *Lateness*, 26, 27, 61, 111, 124; "Limits," 33, 34, 35; "Long Live the Snowflake," 36, 67; "The Lost Golf Ball," 33, 57; *A Man Holding an Acoustic Panel*, 67, 102, 117, 118; "A Man Holding an Acoustic Panel," 18, 117–21, 166; "Master Cantarel at Locus Solus," 81; "Mondrian's Secret," 116 n. 15; "The Mudguard Stroke," 74; "Multiple Suns," 33–34; "Music Written to Order," 107–8; "A Night of Criticism, 42, 43; "The Night Sky," 114; "The Night Sky and to Walter Benjamin," 164; "November Twenty-Seventh," 40, 42; "Ode," 62–63, 66; "The Other and the Others," 112–13, 114; *The Page-Turner*, 114, 140; "The Page-Turner," 79; "Poem," 102–3; *Poems from Deal*, 16, 51, 60, 62, 118, 124; "Poems from Deal," 64–65, 66; *Poets and Painters*, 33, 115, 116 n. 16; "Prayer for a House," 167–68; "Pushkin's Prophet," 131; "Rivulet Near the Truth," 141–42, 148–49; "Screen," 82–83; "The Seasons," 48–49; "Sentences," 44; "The Snow is Alive," 39, 41; "Song of the Eiffel Tower," 48; "Song for Hannah Arendt," 57, 131; "A Song for Rudy Burckhardt," 31, 41–42; "The Sphinx, Again," 114; "Sphinx Skin," 159; "Stay, Stay, Stay, Stay," 145; "A Study of Two Late July Fourths," 157; "Subject (A Song)," 170; "Summer," 115; "Taking a Ferry," 157; "Tall Rock in the Form of an Old Child," 131–35; *To an Idea*, 26, 40, 51, 85, 110, 112, 114, 166; "To an Idea," 26–27, 85–86, 110; "To My Dead Son," 66; "To a Swan," 49–50; "Two-Four Time," 113; "the Uncertainty," 57; "A Visit from the Past," 47; "Venetian Blinds," 79, 140; "A Visit from the Past," 157; "Voice," 31, 55, 98; "A Wall," 111; "Weequahic Park in the Dark," 55–56; "Which Word," 41; "Wild Sonnet," 37–38; "Winter Work," 127–30; "The World in God," 98, 100–101; "Write Out," 114; "You Are Tall and Thin," 22, 27; "You Are the You," 43

Shawn, Wallace, 95
Shlovsky, Victor, 165

Silliman, Ron, 14, 18, 117–22, 124, 180; *In the American Tree*, 124
Sledge, Percy, 159, 161–62
Smith, Stevie: "I Remember," 63, 68 n. 8
Socrates, 95, 150
Sontag, Susan, 169
Speed, 94
Stalin, Joseph, 160
Stein, Gertrude, 111, 124, 171; *Stanzas in Meditation*, 111; *Tender Buttons*, 118
Steinberg, Leo, 70–71, 76; *Other Criteria*, 86 nn. 3, 4, 18, 19, and 22
Stevens, Wallace, 24, 25, 30 n. 6, 62, 68 n. 6, 69, 70, 87 n. 5, 91, 156; "The Emperor of Ice-Cream," 62; "The Noble Rider and the Sound of Words," 25, 30
Stone, Carole, 16, 60–68, 180
Stroffolino, Chris, 116 n. 11
Suleiman, Susan Rubin, 169; "Culture, Aestheticism, and Ethics," 171 n. 7
Swift, Jonathan: *Gulliver's Travels*, 99, 100
Symbolism, French, 19, 87 n. 5, 156, 157

Tabios, Eileen, 136 n. 10
Talisman, 126, 137 n. 12
Thoreau, Henry David, 164; *The Illustrated Walden*, 171 n. 4
Tompkins, Calvin: *Robert Rauschenberg and the Art World of Our Time*, 87 nn. 6 and 7; *The Bride and the Bachelors*, 87 nn. 12–17

Tranter, John: David Shapiro in Conversation with John Tranter, 29, 30 n. 12
Tzu, Chuang, 54

Verlaine, Paul, 158
Vietnam, 17, 121, 130–31

Wachterhauser, Brice, 43; *Beyond Being*, 46 n. 29
Wallace, Mark: "Language and Postlanguage Poetries," 126, 127, 136 n. 3, 137 n. 12
Warhol, Andy, 21, 90, 92
Weill, Simone, 109, 116 n. 10
Whithaus, Carl, 37, 62, 65–66, 68 n. 7, 105; "Immediate Memories," 45 n. 15, 106 nn. 4 and 8
Whitman, Walt, 19, 146–47
Williams, William Carlos, 27, 60, 61, 62, 67, 70, 119; *Imaginations*, 30 n.7; *Kora in Hell*, 118; *Paterson*, 61; "Tract," 67
Wilson, Robert, 124
Wittgenstein, Ludwig, 30, 50
Wordsworth, William: "Lines Composed Above Tintern Abbey," 63

Yau, John, 136, nn. 7 and 10
Yeats, William Butler, 89, 116 n. 11; "Easter, 1916," 89

Ziarek, Krzysztof, 43–44; *Inflected Language*, 46 nn. 33, 34, and 36